Journeying with God

Journeying with God

An Exploration of Ignatian Spirituality

Malcolm Rothwell

EPWORTH PRESS

Copyright © Malcolm A. Rothwell 2001

British Library Cataloguing in Publication data

A catalogue record for this book is available
from the British Library

0 7162 0549 1

First published in 2001
by Epworth Press
20 Ivatt Way
Peterborough PE3 7PG

Typeset in Sabon by MATS, Southend-on-Sea, Essex
and printed in Great Britain by
Biddles Ltd, Guildford and King's Lynn

In loving memory of
my parents
Arthur Rothwell (1913–93)
and
Louie Rothwell (1912–97)
who gave
me a secure and loving foundation.

Contents

Acknowledgments

I am indebted to many people who have assisted me in bringing these personal reflections to fruition:

the late Revd Dr Gordon S. Wakefield, who read my original script and gave much encouragement;

the Revd Gerald M. Burt, editorial secretary of the Epworth Press, and Dr Valerie Edden, a member of the Epworth editorial committee, for their helpful suggestions on content, style and grammar;

Dr Alan and Mrs Freda McIlveen who gave many helpful suggestions after reading my script;

the Revd Andrew Walker, co-director Ignatian Spirituality course, Margaret Street, London, for his expertise and advice;

Sister Ancille Buckley FMDM, for her wisdom and spiritual guidance and the sisters of Ladywell Convent, Godalming, for their prayerful and practical support;

the Revd Phil Hoar, the Revd Brenda Woods and Mrs Yvonne Walker for encouraging me to go on the retreat;

Mrs Helen Oates for telling me about *Hard Times* by Dickens;

the Revd Gerald Reddington who supported and encouraged me through some difficult times;

Mr Bob Russell who kept asking whether I had written a book;

my long-suffering congregations who have listened to countless sermons and taken part in many discussions and those I have been privileged to counsel and offer spiritual direction, but who have taught me so much;

My daughter, Louise Rothwell for patient and painstaking proofreading;

and last, but not least, many thanks to my wife, Lucy, for all her patient help, encouragement and insight.

Preface

It was 10 o'clock in the evening. The day had been gloriously sun-drenched and we had spent the day dipping into the crystal clear waters that surround the beautiful Greek island of Cephelonia. Now the air was only slightly cooler and, of course, there was the constant chorus of crickets singing their songs beneath the star-filled sky. My wife and I had enjoyed three days of exploring this lovely jewel of the Ionian sea.

Then it happened. One minute I was coming out of the bathroom into the bedroom and the next minute I was curled up in pain with a broken leg. In the days that followed as I lay flat on my back I pondered on that wonderful story of Anthony de Mello. 'Good luck? Bad luck? Who knows?' At the time it certainly felt like very bad luck and my wife would agree with that. However there is also that profound and far-reaching text in Romans 8.28: 'We know that in everything God works for good with those who love him, who are called according to his purpose'.

Where was the good in this experience? Gradually the light dawned. The enforced restrictions would allow me the space and the time to write a book about an experience that changed my life. It was precisely that experience which enabled me to see God in everything. God is in all our experiences. The secret is to discern his presence; most of the time we are too busy just surviving and addressing our own agendas. God is simply squeezed out.

Introduction

What on earth was I doing? Could this really be true? Here I was on a cold January day, the New Year parties recently finished, entering a Catholic convent. I was, after all, a Methodist. Was I out of my mind? Had I been working too hard? What would the future hold? What had brought me to this point in time? What was lying in store behind those large oak doors? Could it really be that God was drawing me to this place?

There are times in our lives when we feel drawn to a particular course of action. There seems no obvious rational explanation for this. It just seems the right thing to do. God has put his hand on us. We have experienced, as it were, the divine touch and there it rests. We shall look at this experience more fully in Chapter 8. For the moment let me say that 'touch' first came to me when I was contemplating entering the Methodist ministry. I was a teacher at the time and to make matters more complex, studying for a degree in psychology, and so I was in great doubt as to the precise nature of my call. Furthermore I was concerned that a call is simply theological jargon for a rational decision. Where did motivation come into the decision-making process? Surely other things like early experiences, intellectual assent, Christian faith, came into the equation. There is a complexity of variables that lead up to the critical decision of whether or not to enter the ministry. Nevertheless there was the feeling that I had been gripped by God in a compelling sort of way. The call had come direct from God. It was intimate and sacred. There were

also doubts, strong ones. There were no heavenly voices or
divine bells in the middle of the night. There was no
'scientific' certainty. Anyway, can we only call those
experiences 'acts of God' for which we have no rational
explanation? Is it not true to say that, more often than not,
the word of God is actually mediated to us through the
words, lives and experiences of other people today and as
recorded in the Bible? I hadn't heard of Ignatius, let alone
his rules for discerning whether or not something is of God.
Happily the Methodist Church discerned that my call was
from God and I was accepted for the ministry.

After over 20 years in the ministry it was agreed that I was
due for a sabbatical. As this dream began to get nearer and
become a reality I had to focus on what I could do for three
months without any church commitments. Slowly the idea
began to present itself that I could go on a retreat. A number
of my friends and acquaintances were involved with the
retreat movement and had been on weekend and eight day
Ignatian retreats and spoke of the possibility of a 30-day
retreat. I had begun in my own ministry to spend a day of
silence each month at a retreat centre and found the
experience beneficial. It all seemed to fit. Why not go on a
30-day silent retreat following the Spiritual Exercises of
Ignatius Loyola?[1] As the day for my departure crept ever
nearer I had severe misgivings. What had I let myself in for?
Thirty days of silence felt like a mountain to climb. In my
naivety what did I know about Ignatius except that from my
school history lessons? He was a rather severe soldier and a
Catholic who had founded the Order of Jesuits. What could
a Catholic from the sixteenth century have to say to me, a
Methodist, living in the twentieth century?[2] Was God really
drawing me into this experience? My spiritual director, at an
introductory meeting, had told me not to worry; God was
waiting for me. I was not so sure. However, I made the so-
called leap of faith and entered through the oak doors of the
convent. Thus it was that I embarked on the most intense
and remarkable 30 days of my life.

An invitation, but who from?

I was born towards the middle of the last century, during World War II to be precise. Even in my lifetime there have been far-reaching changes in the world, in society, in the home and also in the church. These changes have impacted on the way we perceive God and the way we think he acts.

Chronologically the year 1900 brought the nineteenth century to its end and marked, at the same time, a climax in the history of its theology with the publication of Harnack's *What is Christianity?* This book represented the greatest expression of bourgeois idealism, an age which was inspired by an optimistic faith in the human mind and progress in history and an age which could look forward with much confidence to the future. Fifteen years later, in August 1914, a manifesto signed by 93 intellectuals of whom Harnack was one signified the collapse of this idealism and optimism. This was certainly felt to be so by the intellectual leaders of the next generation. Forty years later Barth still recalls how:

one day in early August 1914 stands out in my personal memory as a black day. Ninety-three German intellectuals impressed public opinion by their proclamation in support of the war policy of Wilhelm II and his counsellors. Among these intellectuals I discovered to my horror almost all of my theological teachers whom I had greatly venerated. In despair over what this indicated about the signs of the time I suddenly realized that I could not any longer follow either their ethics and dogmatics or their understanding of the bible and of history. For me, at least, nineteenth century theology no longer held any future.[1]

From the historical point of view then, the beginning of the twentieth century is not identical to the year 1900. Historically, the twentieth century began in August 1914 with the outbreak of World War I. This decisive event meant that theology could no longer go on speaking about God in the same way that it had done in the past. Indeed, the question arose as to whether it was possible at all for theologians to speak of God. Barth, however, was anxious to return to the classical faith of the Reformers, a faith, which he maintained, was based unconditionally on God's revelation and not on any human reason or experience. As is well known, Barth took as his starting point not the way we think and speak about God but the way God thinks and speaks about us. Particularly in his early writings we have the imagery of the 'wholly other' breaking in upon humankind 'perpendicularly from above', a disclosure which leads to the 'infinite qualitative distinction' between God and humankind. Barth's conviction that people and human institutions, including institutional religion, are under judgment by the revelation which has broken in on the world led to his theology being described as 'the theology of crisis'.

The far greater horrors of World War II did not produce a similar reaction to those of World War I. The questions now raised tended to be anthropological rather than theological in character: 'How could people do this?' rather than 'How could God allow this?' There was an understandable reticence about reiterating the traditional Christian formulas on the meaning of such events. Indeed, the authenticity and relevance of the Christian faith, as stated in orthodox terms, was seriously questioned. As Zahrnt wrote in the introduction to his book *The Question of God*:

the Christian proclamation, in its traditional form at least, no longer provides the majority of men (*sic*) today with a valid answer to the questions they ask about God, and consequently fails to provide them with an adequate way of understanding their position in the world and of mastering their lives meaningfully.[2]

We have just entered upon not only a new century but a new millennium. In the last hundred years the pace of change has become ever faster. These changes can be seen all around us. Our lives are affected by the computer and, increasingly, by the Internet and the world wide web. We can converse with each other by e-mail without actually talking or without pieces of paper. This can happen almost instantaneously regardless of distance. We can shop over the Internet, book our holidays and carry out a host of other operations. Furthermore we can enter 'virtual reality' whereby we can experience a particular event or situation without actually being there. However, the optimism of previous years in science and technological progress has been replaced with scepticism about whether science has the wherewithal to solve the problems of humankind. The confidence of previous ages has disappeared. In spite of massive scientific advances we still have appalling world poverty, vast numbers of refugees and an increasing desire to solve international problems by the use of violence. In addition, although there have been amazing medical advances, there is the threat of AIDS, cancer is ever present, viruses seem to be ever more resistant to treatment and it is unknown how widespread is the human form of BSE. Small wonder that people ask where is God in all this!

Furthermore, in this so-called post-modern world there is a reluctance to accept any one world view as superior to any other. There is a loss of certainty and identity and a considerable amount of cultural confusion. This is certainly the case for Christians. Whatever happened to Good Friday and Pentecost? Just look at the multiplicity of activities Christians engage in on their supposedly holy days. Ecclesiastical authority has long been questioned and challenged and there are doubts as to whether the Bible can have any relevance for today.[3] There are also those who argue that the church has to find new ways of being the church.[4] In a recent book John Drane writes, 'it must be obvious that the church simply cannot expect to continue to survive for long into the twenty-first century in its present form'.[5] For many the church has become an outmoded edifice, a museum, which has outlived its purposes and must once more be open to where God is taking it. In any event God has no abiding place and God is always greater than the church. However much we may want to control or domesticate him and, as it were, put him in our back pocket, God is always beckoning us on to something new.

I find myself as a citizen of this world, not wanting to reject the world nor wanting to return to a bygone age, but trying to make sense of the world and where God is in it. Christians are often guilty of developing a belief system as though Copernicus, Newton, Darwin, Freud and Einstein had never lived. The theories of these people may be corrected and updated but they cannot be ignored, or their discoveries undone. 'Our religious plight today is that we utilize a Ptolemaic religion within a Copernican universe. Those more attuned to science . . . might prefer to say that we utilize a Newtonian religion within a post-Einstein universe.'[6] There is no doubt that we have to change our ways of thinking about God.[7]

The question is how do we make sense of God in today's world? What kind of spirituality can sustain the Christian pilgrimage? Paradoxically I find myself drawn to a sixteenth-century Spanish mystic, Ignatius Loyola, for insights into the nature of God. Furthermore I have a gut feeling that this God is not an abstract thought, a theoretical construct or figment of my imagination but a reality, just as much as the love of my wife.

This God is not someone who is judging, cajoling or pushing but mystically drawing us into the mystery that he ultimately is. He is the one who invites, who draws us to himself. Many times we can feel driven but it is slaves who are driven. They have no choice. It is forced labour and slaves cannot be forced to love their master. They can only do their duty. Our 'drives' often come from within in terms of what we feel we 'ought' or 'should' do. We end up doing our duty and no more. Commenting on the law of love in Luke's Gospel, G.B. Caird writes, 'Duty is not enough. Duty obeys the rules, but love grasps the opportunities. Duty acts under constraint; love is spontaneous and therefore gracious. Duty expects to be recompensed or at least recognised, love expects nothing in return'.[8]

God does not drive, he invites, and we therefore have to choose whether to accept his invitation. Basically there are two choices: Either we decide to move towards God or we decide to move away. We could, of course, opt to remain stationary but in practice that is very difficult to do. It is difficult because all the time we are making choices and it is these choices that define the direction in which we are travelling. There are choices about how we use our time, and our money, the kind of relationships we want to build on. There are choices about sex, before or after marriage, living together or marrying, about having children or not, pursuing a career, doing the lottery, smoking, drinking large quantities of alcohol or taking other kinds of drugs, going on to further or higher education, engaging in some kind of voluntary work. We even make a choice about whether to get out of bed in the morning. The list is endless and all of us are constantly engaged in making choices. Ultimately the choices we make define us as people and define our philosophy of life. Where is our deepest self engaged? What are the things that bring us to life? From where do we derive our motivation and our creativity? For some these may be the golf course, for others a walk in the hills, digging the garden, cruising on the river, fishing, flower-arranging, knitting and so on. For yet others it may well be formal worship in church on Sundays, especially a celebration of the Lord's Supper. The important thing is that God is a God of Life. He wants us to enjoy life in all its abundance. He is not a God of death. I fear that very often our churches imitate mausoleums or old curiosity shops rather than centres of life-giving energy and too much effort is expended in trying to fan dead ashes into life. When the spark has gone the kindest thing to do is to acknowledge that fact. It is a painful process but, to change the metaphor, the more we prune the dead wood, the more fruit there will be at harvest time.

Ignatius in rather old-fashioned and quaint language talks about our most important choices in terms of the standards, the military banners, of Satan and of Christ,[9] The former 'summons', 'scatters' and 'goads'. People are tempted to 'covet riches so that they may more easily come to vain honour from the world, and finally to surging pride' (##142). According to this first standard riches, honour and pride are the three vices that lead to all others. Coveting riches leads to seeking worldly honour and then to pride. A similar progression may be observed in the temptations of Jesus. It is not that wealth itself is a vice, but that it becomes the means by which Satan ensnares and binds people so that God becomes irrelevant. There is the will to possess and to covet more, the will to be esteemed and to obtain the empty honours of the world and finally the desire to seem very good and to indulge in overweening pride. These desires are ego-driven and the soul is ignored. Here I am, look at what I own; it is all mine.

On the other hand the standard of Christ is to do with 'choosing', 'sending' and 'attracting'. The three steps are quite different. 'The first, poverty as opposed to riches; the second, insults or contempt as opposed to the honour of this world; the third, humility as opposed to pride' (#146). These are the steps which are not only attainable but lead to apostolic service and lead to all other virtues.

Ignatius also suggests that we might contemplate the life of an earthly king (##91) and consider the words of this king.

My will is to conquer the whole land of the infidels. Hence, whoever wishes to come with me has to be content with the same food I eat, and the drink, and the clothing that I wear, and so forth. So too he or she must labour with me during the day, and keep watch in the night, and so on, so that later they may have a part with me in the victory, just as they have shared in the toil. (##93)

This address carries overtones of a crusader mentality and the relationship between a Lord and his vassal. This relationship was often stronger than marriage in those times. The suggestion is that anyone would be foolish to refuse such a generous offer. If such a summons of an earthly king is worth thinking about 'how much more worthy of consideration it is to look on Christ our Lord, the eternal King'. He states, 'my will is to conquer the whole world and all my enemies, and thus to enter into the glory of my Father. Therefore, whoever wishes to come with me must labour with me, so that through following me in the pain he or she may follow me also in the glory' (##95).

This distinction between the two standards or banners of Satan and Christ and the meditation on the call of the king were not for Ignatius a theoretical discussion. They arose from the crucible of his own experience.

The name Ignatius was not actually used until he was middle-aged. He was born in 1491 in the Spanish town of Loyola and was actually baptized Inigo. He was born into a noble family and was trained as a page for service in important households and even in the king's court although he himself was never appointed a royal page. However he did grow up within an environment in which ideals of courtesy, honour, truthfulness and fidelity were paramount. While Inigo was still a young man, his patron fell on hard times for disobeying the new king Emperor Charles V. Inigo soon found himself serving as a soldier. In 1521 he was in the army at Pamplona, facing the French invaders. A cannonball seriously injured Inigo's leg.

Inigo was well treated by the French, but he required two operations on his leg. In fact a third one was necessary because he was still unable to wear the close fitting tights that were then fashionable for men. This third operation Inigo deliberately chose. Clearly he had a very high pain threshold. There were no anaesthetics. During a long convalescence he began to read the only books that were available. These were not romantic novels, as he would have wished, but *The Life of Christ* and *The Lives of the Saints*. This convalescence became the first major turning point in his life. Instead of dreaming about becoming a great warrior and winning the hand of some fair lady, he began to dream about following Christ in great hardship. He discovered that the latter dreams gave him a feeling of contentment whereas the former dreams of deeds of chivalry left him sad and discontented. The conclusion that Inigo drew from this was that the dreams of Christ were inspired by God whereas the other dreams were not. Inigo used the terminology of good and bad spirits. It has been argued that it was this discernment of different spirits that began the conversion of Inigo.

In brief, Inigo began to feel that Jesus Christ as a king with a kingdom was far more important than the Spanish king and his kingdom whom he had been serving. Moreover he had been greatly moved by the lives of the saints about whom he had been reading. He found them to be brave and marvellous people and he wanted to be a follower of Christ in the spirit of the saints. Thus it was that Inigo began a life of poverty and he embarked on a ministry preaching about the kingdom of God.

In Chapter 8 we shall look at the question of discernment

and how we discover the will of God. For the moment suffice it to say that Inigo discovered within himself that we are often pulled in opposing directions. For many of us the main pull is towards ourselves – our wants, our achievements, our successes, our status, our egos. We are number one and the earth revolves around us. It was Copernicus in the fifteenth century who discovered that the sun does not revolve around the earth but vice versa; the earth revolves around the sun. This was a major revolution in people's thinking at that time. The earth was thought to be the centre of the whole universe. Copernicus was not popular and met a great deal of opposition.

In similar fashion we can vehemently oppose such a Copernican revolution in our own lives. God and his creation do not revolve around us but vice versa. We and creation revolve around God. Thus we are presented with a challenge. Can we cease being self-centred, preoccupied with building our own kingdom or can we change our focus, our direction, and become God-centred and start to build the kingdom of God? Margaret Silf has written about this in a very imaginative, well-illustrated book. She explains that when we are moving away from God who is the Light, we have our backs to him and a shadow falls in front of us.

> My own bulk (which is just an image for my 'ego') will overshadow all that I do – all my efforts, all my relationships, all my journey. Not only will I not be able to see the way ahead, because of my own shadow, but it will cast the darkness over others. I will make the world a darker place. And, of course, the bigger my ego, the larger and darker will be the shadow I cast.[10]

Moreover that shadow can fall over other people as well. Silf uses the example that many of us heard as children when we were told off by parents for 'sitting in our own light'. We were mystified at the time but now it makes sense. In our own light the vision is restricted because brightness is reduced. We thought we could manage. We wanted to stay in control. The earth, as it were, revolved around us and so, we assumed, did other planets.

On the other hand if we are directed towards God, the source of Light, the shadow falls behind us. We are moving towards the sun and the feelings within us are quite different. No longer do we feel alienated and troubled. There is a feeling of peace and harmony. Sometimes, just sometimes, we actually get things right. We know we have made the right decision. We know we have not been driven by our own selfish desires. We have made our decision in the light of the love of God. It feels right. We have been granted a brief glimpse of what life is ultimately all about. It could be said that the Spiritual Exercises of Ignatius are a way in which we might begin to move more fully towards God. In fact Ignatius starts his Exercises with his First Principle and Foundation: 'Human beings are created to praise, reverence, and serve God our Lord, and by this means to save their souls' (##23). Before examining further these Exercises, let me fill in some more details of the life of Inigo.

At the age of 26 Inigo left his brother's castle where he had been convalescing and went to the town of Manresa. It was here, mainly in a cave, that he spent about eight months in intense prayer and ascetic exercises. His prayers began to change. For example he began to think of Gospel events and try to make himself present in each scene. He would be present, say, at the Last Supper or in the stable at Bethlehem and watch, listen and talk to those present. This method of praying with the Scriptures is an important theme in the Exercises.

We shall return at some length to this method of praying at a later stage. For the moment suffice it to say that Inigo wrote notes during his time at Manresa and these became the basis of his Spiritual Exercises. He began to direct others through these Exercises. Of course there was a good deal of opposition by the recognized clergy because Inigo was not ordained as a priest. The Exercises were officially approved by the Pope in 1548.

Inigo spent the years after Manresa travelling about in Italy and France, usually on foot and usually begging his way. He also went to the Holy Land. He spent time in colleges and universities trying to improve his education. At the age of 43 three Inigo passed his final examination for the Arts degree at the University of Paris. The secretaries who filled in his certificate thought that the Latin for Inigo must be Ignatius, which is what they wrote. Henceforth Inigo was known as Ignatius from Loyola. During this time he gathered a company of friends round him who were attracted to his way of life. The most famous of these is probably Francis Xavier who also came from a noble family. In the course of time they called themselves Companions of Jesus which in Latin is *socii Jesu*. This was translated into English as the Society of Jesus or Jesuits. They were eventually officially recognized by the Pope as an order within the Roman Catholic Church.

It is important to point out that this group of people in the first instance was nearly all laymen at the time of making the Exercises. In other words they were not designed for those who had taken to the priesthood or were members of religious orders or for especially holy people. They were written for people who simply wanted to deepen their relationship with God and know, serve and love him better. Ignatius was ordained in 1537. He died in 1556. Now it is time to look more closely at the Exercises.

The Spiritual Exercises of Ignatius Loyola (the Exercises)

The Exercises are divided into four 'weeks' although the word 'week' is misleading. Ideally one spends about 30 days in solitude away from the distractions of daily life and these 30 days are divided into four phases or stages which may be longer or shorter than seven days. Between each phase there is a transitional or repose day when the retreatant is allowed a measure of relaxation. During the course of each day there are five one-hour sessions of quiet prayer or meditation usually based on a passage of scripture. After each session of prayer, the retreatant has a time of reflection and making notes and these become the basis of a personal interview at some stage each day with a spiritual director whose counsel helps to interpret the events of each day. It is the spiritual director whose task it is to decide when each phase or 'week' is completed although one could argue that ultimately it is God who is the director. 'The director can only watch to see how God will direct this particular retreatant.'[11]

The Exercises have been described as a 'conversation between personal experience and the story of the gospels'[12] for, undoubtedly, it is the events of the life of Jesus which are the focus of the meditations. Ignatius himself had gone back to the life of Christ when he lay wounded in Loyola and it was there that he discovered the will of God for himself. The retreatant is invited to imitate this process and thus discover what the will of God is. The Exercises therefore constitute Ignatius' 'greatest contribution to the formation of adult Christian believers'.[13] Just as one needs physical exercise in order to keep the body in shape, these Exercises are designed to tone up one's spiritual life.

During the first week the retreatant is asked to reflect on his or her sins and sinful tendencies in order that the love and goodness of God may be revealed. The second week is based on a contemplation of the life of Christ. The incarnation, birth and public ministry of Jesus are the focus of prayer and reflection. In the third week the retreatant is invited to identify as closely as possible with the passion of Jesus, his suffering and death. The fourth week centres on the resurrection of Jesus.

In brief, the Exercises offer a profound opportunity to encounter God. This was perhaps the unconscious motivation for my deciding to make the retreat in the first place. This came home to me with great force during my first

walk. Each day I went for a walk in the surrounding
countryside. Although there were five sessions of formal
prayer, I found that God also spoke clearly in the informal
moments between the set times for prayer.[14]

I set off for this walk not having the faintest idea where
I was going. It seemed to be appropriate to go where the
Spirit directed. This was to be the pattern for future walks
although, obviously, the surrounding countryside became
more familiar day by day. The fact that I had entered upon
this retreat having very little idea where I was going or
where I would end up is an obvious parallel to draw.
However I stuck to well-worn paths and therefore
presumed that I would not get lost. In the same way many
thousands of people have followed the well-worn paths of
the Exercises and lived to tell the tale.

In the distance I saw an intriguing farmhouse. From afar
it looked a really solid, well-built structure. As I drew near
it became obvious that the house was derelict. The
windows were broken. The house was empty. It was not
lived in. The precise state of the building was only apparent
from close inspection. The thought occurred that this
house was remarkably like my spiritual state. I certainly
felt well built on the outside and the foundations were
secure but what was on the inside?[15] I was feeling like an
empty shell or to use another metaphor the well was
running dry. The irony of this is that I had recently
preached on the text 'every one who drinks of this water
will thirst again, but whoever drinks of the water that I
shall give him will become in him a spring of water gushing
up to eternal life' (John 4.13). I was reminded of the
following dialogue in *The Silver Chair* by C.S. Lewis:

'Are you not thirsty?', said the Lion.
'I'm *dying* of thirst', said Jill.
'Then drink', said the Lion.
'May I – could I – would you mind going away while I
do?', said Jill.

The Lion answered this only by a look and a very low growl. And as Jill gazed at its motionless bulk, she realized that she might as well have asked the whole mountain to move aside for her convenience.

The delicious rippling noise of the stream was driving her nearly frantic.

'Will you promise not to – do anything to me, if I do come?', said Jill.

'I make no promise', said the Lion.

Jill was so thirsty now that, without noticing it, she had come a step nearer.

'*Do* you eat girls?', she said.

'I have swallowed up girls and boys, women and men, kings and emperors, cities and realms', said the Lion. It didn't say this as if it were boasting, nor as if it were sorry, nor as if it were angry. It just said it.

'I daren't come and drink', said Jill.

'Then you will die of thirst', said the Lion.

'Oh dear!', said Jill, coming another step nearer. 'I suppose I must go and look for another stream then.'

'There is no other stream', said the Lion.[16]

Now I knew why I had come on the retreat. I needed to drink from the living water. It was time to recharge my batteries if not to completely refit my spiritual life. The question was, 'Would the Exercises meet my needs or would I be feeling just as empty at the end of 30 days?' There were lots of questions, apprehensions and uncertainties during this first walk. Little did I know the surprises that were in store. A slight encouragement at this stage was that on the walk I found myself standing in the middle of a very large field. This really was a wide open space across which a cold wind was blowing. However, on closer inspection the field was full of small green shoots. Could it be that there were signs of growth within me even at this stage?

2

Jottings on prayer

Clearly the Exercises depend on prayer, a great deal of it. More specifically there are five set periods of prayer per day lasting approximately one hour each. One could argue that the whole retreat takes place within the context of prayer. Even going for a walk, one is aware of the silence. It is the constant silence and quietness that gives a heightened sense of awareness and the opportunity to listen to God. This was a relatively new experience. Prayer is often experienced as the need to say the right words, whatever they may be, as though we can only talk to God in some kind of religious jargon. Not only is it imagined that we need the right words but also a lot of them. Our prayers tend to be a shopping list of requests that we lay at the door of God in the hope he will answer them in the ways that we want and we become frustrated if he doesn't. If nothing seems to happen we quickly become fed up and think the whole exercise is a waste of time. Of course, sometimes nothing does seem to happen but the point is that we are being available to God. Prayer, after all, is not for God's benefit, it is for our well-being. Prayer is not so much telling God what to do as listening for him to tell us what to do. As when we love someone, we are attentive to their needs so in prayer we pay attention to God. Again, as when we love someone this attention may simply, indeed, most profoundly be when we gaze at our beloved and they gaze at us.

Since God speaks through his creation and human beings are part of that creation, it stands to reason that he is able to speak to us and through us. For this to happen we have to be receptive and that demands silence. This is not silence in the negative sense of the absence of noise, this is silence in the positive sense of being receptive and quiet.

There is no doubt that the last few years have seen an increase in people looking for silence. Proof of this is found in the great interest shown in the retreat movement. 'The discovery of silence is accompanied by the discovery of solitude.'[1] This is not the same as being lonely. Solitude is something that is deliberately chosen. It is a time to be used creatively with God. For better or for worse we live in a time where we are bombarded with an enormous barrage of stimulation. Our senses become dulled by the amount of information we receive. Our brains find it difficult to process all the data that they are assaulted with. We have become accustomed to background music and background noise wherever we are. A retreat is a time of solitude and silence.

One of the disciplines that has to be acquired in the Exercises is the ability to be quiet. Silent prayer is not the same as doing nothing. I find it relatively easy to do nothing: 'Sometimes I sits and thinks, and then again I just sits' (*Punch*, 1906). However to pray in silence is quite another thing because of the multitude of distractions, which impinge on us and take us away from the task of listening to what God is saying. We shall return shortly to the subject of distractions but first let us consider the question of silence.

Silent prayer

I well remember one of my earliest services as a preacher. I incorporated a few minutes of silent reflection into the order of service. The total time spent in this way could not have been more than two or three minutes but towards the end I distinctly heard a member of the congregation say, 'I think he has gone to sleep.' Silent prayer is not easy. During the retreat there was nothing but silence. I ate in silence, went for a walk in silence, prayed in silence and everything else was in silence. There was no background noise in the form of radio or television, nor was there a conversation with anyone except with my spiritual director for roughly one hour per day. I well remember that on my first repose day during my evening meal I was allowed to listen to some music. Never has Beethoven's *Eroica* symphony sounded more wonderful. The music immediately refocused my attention. The silence which had sometimes become oppressive was now broken.

Of course there are different kinds of silence. Silence can be cold, angry or embarrassing. It can be born out of awkwardness and uncertainty or compromise or acquiescence. There is the silence of safety and conformity. Silence can also be very threatening. This latter feeling is perhaps the most common since in extended silence we can be put in touch with our innermost feelings and these are sometimes quite painful. All those who are involved in counselling or therapy know the value of silence. Indeed at one level counselling could be described as the art of interpreting silences.

Freud and Jung were among the earliest psychologists who sought to uncover the deep recesses of the unconscious. These recesses are normally hidden from us because of our defence mechanisms. However in silence these defences become weaker and we become more sensitive to material in the unconscious. For this reason, as Denis Duncan points out, silence may not be appropriate for everyone. 'If we have the inner strength and security to cope . . . the experience can be a creative one. But if our "defences" are down, we may simply be overwhelmed by the kind of thoughts we are getting and consequently "break down".'[2]

It is not surprising that we try to fill our silences with words. The following is quoted in a book of prayers and it comes from South India.

A friend of mine, a Japanese missionary in Thailand, has among his acquaintances a few deeply religious Buddhist monks. On one occasion they decided to enter into theological discussion, and as part of the process resolved to study together their respective scriptures. One of the books they chose was St. John's gospel. So, one day they began the study of John, and started with the first verse of the first chapter, 'In the beginning was the Word.'

'My,' said one of the Buddhists monks, 'even in the beginning you Christians didn't have a little time for silence!'

There is no doubt about it that those of other faiths often find us Christians a noisy and boisterous people, with no great depth to us, and very little time for quiet.[3]

To put this slightly differently we are in danger of speaking 'words in order not to hear the Word which comes out of silence'.[4]

In his classic book of prayers Michel Quoist uses everyday objects and situations as a focus. This is his meditation called 'the telephone'.

I have just hung up; why did he telephone?
I don't know . . . Oh! I get it . . .
I talked a lot and listened very little.

Forgive me, Lord, it was a monologue, and not a dialogue.
I explained my idea and did not get his;
Since I didn't listen, I learned nothing,
Since I didn't listen, I didn't help,
Since I didn't listen, we didn't communicate.

Forgive me, Lord, for we were connected,
and now we are cut off.[5]

In his seminal book on prayer Hans Urs von Balthasar writes about prayer as being communication with God. This is not new but we often fail to realize the implications. 'Prayer . . . is communication in which God's word has the initiative and we, at first, are simply listeners. Consequently, what we have to do is, first, listen to God's word and then, through that word, learn how to answer.'[6] This idea of listening is all very well in theory but many feel uncomfortable with it and even say they can't do it. Some would even say that the metaphor of God on the other end of a telephone line is not a helpful one. The image may have helped people in the past:

> but it is now so alien to their experience of God that they find it too embarrassing to use, even as an image. The God they have experienced is in no sense a telephone answering service providing neat answers to the questions they put. They not only want to accept responsibility for their own decisions; they know they would have to even if they didn't want to, for the hotline to heaven has gone dead.[7]

It is as though 'there is no one there. The conversation I have with him, that conversation with one voice, and one way only, is the monologue of a half-wit in his padded cell.'[8]

Whatever kind of prayer we use there must always be a sense of responsibility. Prayer is not a means by which we ask God to do things we are perfectly able to do ourselves. The reason why the 'hotline has gone dead' is because the ability to listen in an increasingly noisy world is extremely difficult. Balthasar with impeccable logic says that 'since God himself has made us such that, to be truly ourselves, we have to listen to his word, he must, for that reason, have endowed us with the ability to do so; otherwise, he would be in contradiction with himself and so not be the truth.'[9]

Thomas Merton is arguably the most well-known monk of the twentieth century. For many years he lived in a hermitage near to a monastery and, not surprisingly, he draws on the experience of the monastic tradition. In one of his books on prayer he gives this quotation from a Syrian monk, Isaac of Nineveh.

Many are avidly seeking but they alone find who remain in continual silence ... Every man who delights in a multitude of words, even though he says admirable things, is empty within. If you love truth, be a lover of silence. Silence like the sunlight will illuminate you in God and will deliver you from the phantoms of ignorance. Silence will unite you to God himself ...

More than all things love silence: it brings you a fruit that tongue cannot describe. In the beginning we have to force ourselves to be silent. But then there is born something that draws us to silence. May God give you an experience of this 'something' that is born of silence. If only you practise this, untold light will dawn on you in consequence ... after a while a certain sweetness is born in the heart of this exercise and the body is drawn almost by force to remain in silence.[10]

During the fourth century AD the deserts of Egypt, Palestine, Arabia and Persia were inhabited by men who had abandoned the pagan world in search of salvation. These were the Desert Fathers, the first Christian hermits. Merton has compiled a collection of their sayings. 'A monk ought not to inquire how this one acts, or how that one lives. Questions like this take us away from prayer and draw us on to backbiting and chatter. There is nothing better than to keep silent.'[11]

'Any trial whatever that comes to you can be conquered by silence.'[12] This is reminiscent of Jesus standing silent before Pilate. These sentiments are reinforced by another mystic Thomas à Kempis. 'In silence and in stillness a religious soul advantageth itself, and learneth the mysteries of Holy Scripture.'[13]

It is not just that we learn the mysteries of Scripture, in silence we also come to a knowledge of ourselves. We expose ourselves to God who knows us better than we know ourselves. In silence we are naked before God. Julian of Norwich wrote in the fourteenth century 'God is nearer to us than our own soul, for he is the ground in which it stands, and his the means by which substance and sensuality are so held together that they can never separate'.[14]

As we have seen, the therapeutic process uses silence as one of its main instruments. However, once the initial anxiety has been overcome: 'the good analyst, like the wise teacher of the desert, knows that silence leads to life and acceptance. For the mature teacher, silence is nothing less than the expression of his particular way of being.'[15] It is common knowledge that women are much more likely to seek counselling than men. Indeed they are much more likely to attend church. This could be because they are much more comfortable with silence. The use of words could be seen to be a masculine trait, a way of dominating and controlling.

'Speech is masculine: it goes out and penetrates, in order to give pleasure and impregnate. The seed longs for the earth . . . Through the word I put my semen inside another person . . . Hearing is feminine. The ear is a void, waiting for the word which will bring pleasure and life.'[16] This same writer, Rubem Alves, also writes about the soul as being a void. In silence we can begin to get in touch with the fact that this void is also the place where God can be found.

The inward journey

T.S. Eliot writes, 'we must be still and still moving into another intensity for a further union, a deeper communion.'[17] This is the ultimate aim of silence, to move into a deeper communion with God whom we find at the heart of our being.

The words used to describe this kind of prayer can some-times be confusing. It is sometimes called meditation and sometimes contemplation. In the last analysis it is a form of prayer in which the individual becomes aware that he or she is in the presence of God. Words are not necessary and may even become a hindrance. As the psalmist says, 'Be still, and know that I am God!'(Psalm 46.10). The hymn writer offers a similar sentiment:

Drop thy still dews of quietness,
Till all our strivings cease;
Take from our souls the strain and stress,
And let our ordered lives confess
The beauty of thy peace.[18]

For Teresa of Avila the journey of prayer is an inward journey. 'If we took care to recollect what a Guest we have within us, I think it would be impossible to give ourselves so much to the things of this world, because we should realize how base they are in comparison with what we possess in our souls.'[19] Consequently growth in prayer is a growth inwards. St John of the Cross says that God is a quietly burning flame at the centre of our being. 'Contem-plation is nothing less than a secret, peaceful and loving infusion from God. When it is allowed to, it lights the soul with the spirit of love.'[20] Thomas Merton writes, 'the aim of meditation, in the context of Christian faith, is not to arrive at an objective and apparently "scientific" know-ledge about God, but to come to know him through the realization that our very being is penetrated with his knowledge and love for us'.[21] 'Contemplation is essentially a listening in silence, an expectancy.'[22]

The method requires an 'inner surrendering of our own mind and heart to God'[23] so that we can reach him at a deeper level of our consciousness. This is the Christ of the heart, what St Augustine calls the 'inner teacher'. It is 'God's interior truth that enlightens me, is something fundamentally other than the "depths of my soul", than my archetypes and profoundest categories, classifications and ideals.'[24] To this extent God is nearer to us than we are to ourselves. He is nearer than our own breathing. 'The truth, which is the Spirit dwelling in us, is more interior to us than we are to ourselves.'[25] Julian of Norwich says, 'prayer brings about the union between God and man's soul'.[26] In other words prayer unites the soul to God, or prayer 'ones the soul to God'.[27]

Thomas Merton writes in a similar vein:

> The contemplative has nothing to tell you except to reassure you and say that if you dare to penetrate your own silence and risk the sharing of that solitude with the lonely other who seeks God through you, then you will truly recover the light and the capacity to understand what is beyond words and beyond explanations because it is too close to be explained: it is the intimate union in the depths of your own heart, of God's own spirit and your own secret inmost self, so that you and He are in all truth One Spirit.[28]

Thus, in meditation, we are not trying to find out about God, as though it were an exercise in analytic thought. We are trying to know God in himself. God is not an object among others. God is apprehended with the heart through faith. 'True contemplation is not a psychological trick but a theological grace. It can come to us *only* as a gift, and not as a result of our own clever use of spiritual techniques.'[29]

Clearly, though, some kind of attentiveness is needed. A notable mystic of the last century, Simone Weil writes that prayer 'is the orientation of all the attention of which the soul is capable towards God. The quality of the attention counts for much in the quality of the prayer. Warmth of heart cannot make up for it.'[30] Neville Ward also talks about attention:

Contemplation is the way into prayer for most people in our generation. They should begin here, by being thankful, by being attentive to the experience they enjoy, by endeavouring to hold themselves quietly and apprecia-tively in the presence of the good which is pleasing them, and by holding themselves there as long as they can.[31]

However this kind of attention is far from easy. 'The soul never remains static as it travels on the road of contemplation as it is always rising or falling.'[32] This brings us to the question of distractions during times of silence for this kind of prayer demands a high level of concentration and attentiveness.

Distractions

When making a retreat it is clear that a lot of external distractions have been reduced to a minimum. There are no demands from the family; there is no shopping to be done; there is no telephone; there is no doorbell and there are no newspapers so one cannot be distracted by current affairs or the state of the national sports teams. However I was well aware of all kinds of internal diversions. Sometimes other people would be praying in the same room and I could focus on them. It was a great temptation to look out of the window and begin to daydream. There was often the aroma of cooking emanating from the kitchen and I would begin to wonder what was for dinner. There were times of boredom and I wondered when the hour of prayer would finish. My watch would then provide a focus. Another ploy would be when studying a particular passage of Scripture to look up all the footnotes and compare and contrast the set passage with other similar passages. Another fear was that of thinking that God would never have anything to say to me and that the whole hour of prayer would be a complete waste of time. The amazing thing is that this rarely, if ever, happened.

All of these, and many more, were methods my mind employed to disturb the concentration and take away the business of the present moment. It is precisely when there is a distraction that one has to check whether it is a red herring or whether the diversion has to be pursued. God can just as easily speak through the side dishes as through the main course. Gerard Hughes writes, 'there is, therefore, nothing in creation, no experience of life, which is necessarily a distraction. Everything that happens to us is an invitation from God to turn to him. So prayer is as wide as creation: there is no experience which cannot become a prayer.'[33] After all, our experiences, the things that happen to us, are one of the means God employs to speak to us. The best way of denying God is to deny our experience.

Of course, there is nothing new in our human ability to be easily distracted. Centuries ago Teresa of Avila wrote,

for more than fourteen years, I was never able even to meditate without the aid of a book. Many people must be in like case, and there are others, who even with reading, cannot make a meditation, but use vocal prayers, which keep them more recollected. Some have such a lively imagination, that they cannot fix their thoughts on one subject, but they are always wandering, and to such an extent, that when these persons wish to think of God, a thousand vain fancies, scruples and doubts arise in their minds.[34]

There is some encouragement from that fact that this is a common problem but if we find ourselves feeling guilty or uncomfortable about distractions then we have to return gently and repeatedly to the act of listening to God in the present moment. Only when all the background noise, both internal and external, has been eliminated can we really be available to listen to God. This is the purpose of prayer; allowing God to enter into a situation so that we can achieve union with him and seek his will.

Sometimes it is very hard work and sometimes it just happens. Sometimes we have to search long and hard for water and even dig a well. Sometimes we find a stream or a river. Sometimes it rains! This was certainly my experience. There were times of hard, concentrated effort and at other times everything fell into place. It was as though I had been 'brushed by a butterfly's wing'.[35]

The major distraction is wondering if you are ever going to get there. Sometimes the future looks like a massive mountain to be climbed and you cannot possibly imagine that you will ever arrive. The other tendency is to be distracted by the past and to rest, as it were, on one's laurels and to bathe in past glories or wallow in past misdemeanours. Both of these tendencies detract from the present moment. The tendency is summed up in the following passage that is worth quoting at length:

To the untrained eye ego-climbing and selfless climbing may appear identical. Both kinds of climbers place one foot in front of the other. Both breathe in and out at the same time. Both stop when tired. Both go forward when rested. But what a difference! The ego-climber is like an instrument that is out of adjustment. He puts his foot down an instant too soon or too late. He's likely to miss a beautiful passage of sunlight through the trees. He goes on when the sloppiness of his step shows he's tired. He rests at odd times. He looks up the trail to see what's ahead even when he knows what's ahead because he just looked a second before. He goes too fast or too slow for the conditions and when he talks his talk is forever about somewhere else, something else. He's here but he's not here. He rejects the here, is unhappy with it, wants to be farther up the trail but when he gets there will be just as unhappy because then *it* will be 'here'. What he's looking for, what he wants, is all around him, but he doesn't want that because it *is* all around him. Every step's an effort, both physically and spiritually, because he imagines his goal to be external and distant.[36]

Learning to listen to God in every moment is a discipline to be learnt. It means shifting the attention from what I am doing in any one moment of time to being attentive to what God is saying in that moment. The difficulty lies in the fact that we spend a lot of our time planning for the future, the next meal, the next sermon, the next meeting, future holidays and events and so on. As a minister I find my life geared to, and almost dictated by, a diary. Without my diary I have sometimes felt that my world would fall apart. Thus the present moment escapes us. 'The fugitive moment refuses to stay.'[37] Somebody has said that life is something that happens to us while we are busy making plans. Anthony de Mello calls such an attitude 'pathetic'.[38] Of course, it goes without saying that some planning is necessary for everyday living. However, the present moment is all we have. The past has gone and we can do nothing about it however much we would like to, the future has not yet arrived, and indeed, may not arrive at all.

In the New Testament there are two Greek words which are used for time. *Chronos* refers to the passing of time. This is to do with the calendar and with dates and, obviously, the word chronology is derived from it. On the other hand, *kairos* refers to God's time, the time of opportunity and decision. In a profound sense all time is God's time, but to achieve this state of looking at life is something only the saints have achieved.

J.-P. de Caussade calls this way of thinking the sacrament of the present moment:

It is necessary to be disengaged from all we feel and do in order to walk with God in the duty of the present moment. All other avenues are closed. We must confine ourselves to the present moment without taking thought for the one before or the one to come.[39]

To have achieved such a state of disengagement would be almost impossible. Furthermore to deny what we are doing and feeling, it seems to me, would be to deny the activity of God for surely he often speaks to us precisely through what we are doing and thinking. The most common way of denying God is to deny our experience. Nevertheless the thrust of de Caussade's thinking is clear. 'The present moment holds infinite riches beyond your wildest dreams but you will only enjoy them to the extent of your faith and love . . . the will of God is manifest in each moment.'[40] The emphasis of this approach is clear. All we need to know is God's will for us in each moment of time, in the here and now. To this extent 'no moment is trivial since each one contains a divine kingdom, and heavenly sustenance'.[41]

Anthony de Mello gives the following illustration:

The Japanese warrior was captured by his enemies and thrown into prison. At night he could not sleep for he was convinced that he would be tortured the next morning. Then the words of his master came to his mind. 'Tomorrow is not real. The only reality is now.' So he came to the present and fell asleep.[42]

In theory this is all very well but the practice is very different. The present is 'an exceedingly slippery customer. It changes its colour, its shape, its content, minute by minute. All of us are aware of the present moment, yet none of us can define it. It won't wait to be examined or analysed.'[43] This slipperiness was certainly in evidence during my retreat. Although external distractions had been cut down to a minimum the brain was always finding ways of fleeing from the present, especially when the going got tough. Not a day passed when, at some stage, I could have cheerfully gone back home. Philip Sheldrake gives the example of someone who was making the 30-day retreat but refused to pay the bill in full. Each morning she visited the bursar's office and paid just enough money for the next 24 hours. She could not commit herself to more than one day at a time until she was ready to.[44]

Of course, this way of living 'one day at a time' is not new. Jesus exhorts his followers not to 'worry about tomorrow, for tomorrow will bring worries of its own. Today's trouble is enough for today'(Matthew 6.34). During the early days of my retreat, I remember going for a walk and constantly repeating that phrase to myself: 'one day at a time'. As soon as I tried to look too far ahead the clouds descended and anxiety took over. To make the effort of listening to God in each moment was a new skill for me. I had never been taught, or had it explained to me, that this was of the essence of prayer. At theological college my tutors had concentrated on making sure I had the tools of theological enquiry and the instruments of biblical criticism and historical analysis. It was just assumed that I knew how to pray. Certainly since becoming a minister no one has ever asked me about the condition of my prayer life. In all honesty I would sometimes have replied that it was rather less than satisfactory.

On another occasion I was walking through a field and a bird was on the path in front of me. As I approached the bird flew ahead and again alighted on the path. Once more, as soon as I came closer, the bird flew off. This process was repeated a few times before the bird finally flew off into the skies. This gave me an image of how God works. We have our dreams and our visions for the future and these are vital for our well-being. Indeed without them, as the writer of Proverbs says in the Authorized Version, 'we perish' (Proverbs 29.18). However, we have to be ready at any time to change that vision. God is a 'beckoning God'[45] who draws us into the future but he only shows us enough of his will for the present moment. To want to have everything cut and dried, natural though it is, implies that we are trying to control God. Yet God is a God of surprises and the Spirit constantly blows where it wills.

We are assured of the fact that God gives us just enough bread for each day. 'Give us this day our daily bread.' Indeed as the children of Israel discovered in the wilderness, the manna they received would not last more than a day. They were specifically instructed to collect just sufficient manna for each day.

This was the major lesson I learnt in the early days of my retreat: To take each day one at a time and sometimes each one hour at a time in the knowledge that God gives us sufficient strength for that. It is an important lesson to learn especially for those who are going through a difficult period of loss or separation or bereavement. The mountain that lies ahead can only be traversed a step at a time, not in one mighty jump of which we are incapable. This was the frame of mind I adopted throughout the retreat and, although I didn't know it at the time, it was this strategy which enabled me to live through some very dark days that lay ahead later in the year when I went through the trauma of divorce.

3

The need for forgiveness – a personal account

During the first few days of my retreat I was forcibly struck by how alone I felt. Although surrounded by a community of sisters, I was very much on my own. I did not engage in conversation with anyone except a daily session with my director. All my meals I ate alone, in silence. This was an almost totally new experience. As a minister I am used to being in demand. The ministerial role is such that there are always things to do – letters to write, services to plan, people to visit, phone calls to answer, administration to be dealt with and meetings to prepare for. On a silent retreat the agenda is totally different. Indeed the very word agenda betrays how my time is usually spent at business meetings; it is singularly inappropriate in this context. This was an environment in which God was free to organize his own agenda and not be constrained by mine. So many times we treat God as though he were in our back pocket, neatly contained and controlled. So many times we have our hands full, so that God can't put anything in them. So many times we are too busy to create the space for God.

I could hear the phone ringing in the distance and felt the distinct urge to go and answer it. The doorbell would ring, but nobody ever came for me. There was a message board for the sisters in the community, but there was never any message for me. The postman arrived, but there were never any letters for me. (I was only allowed to receive messages and make telephone calls on my rest days.) There were no newspapers or music or television and I was only allowed to read a book on a rest day. There was even a party for the festival of Epiphany when a group of Franciscan friars came to celebrate with the sisters, but I was not invited. I had to celebrate on my own with a lovely meal and a glass of wine. I felt totally alone. Nobody wanted me. Is this what retirement or old age is like? How do people cope with the feeling of not being needed? How does one prepare for such an experience?

Strangely enough a few weeks before making the retreat a member of my congregation had put into my hands a copy of Terry Waite's book about his experiences as a hostage in Beirut.[1] From there I was led on to read Brian Keenan's experiences in a similar situation.[2] I found these books to be very helpful in my solitude although, of course, my experience could hardly be compared. To think of my experience and theirs in the same breath cannot really be justified. The hostages were not there voluntarily. They had no choice in where they stayed, what they ate or wore. They were totally at the mercy of their captors. Moreover they had no way of knowing when their captivity would end. All they could do was live from day to day or minute to minute with acute uncertainty, not knowing whether their enforced captivity would ever end or whether, indeed, their lives would come to an abrupt end. The major similarity was the silence. The knowledge that other people were around but there could be no contact with them. If Waite and Keenan and the other hostages had survived their terrible ordeal, surely I could survive the next 29 days in circumstances which, in comparison, were luxurious.

There is a sense in which we are alone in the world. We come into the world on our own and we shall leave the world on our own. I have become more and more convinced about the fragility of our human life. Sometimes it feels as though our human lives are 'hanging by a thread'. At any moment our mortal lives may end, just as children we may be thoroughly enjoying ourselves playing with our friends and then there is the parental call that it is time for bed. Yet we can become so involved with our own worlds and so full of our own importance that we fail to appreciate the fragility of life. 'Naked I came from my mother's womb, and naked I shall return there' (Job 1.21). The lives of the vast majority of people will be forgotten in two or three generations, if not before. Not many have the gifts of a Shakespeare, a Beethoven, a Newton, a Picasso, or indeed of a St Paul. One of the more sobering aspects of the retreat was the knowledge that not only was my church functioning without me but so was the world. We might imagine that we are indispensable but the reality is quite the opposite. The world continues to go about its business with or without us, and at a more mundane level, *Coronation Street* and *Eastenders* will still appear on the television.

In fact it was a truly chastening experience to come out of the retreat and discover that my family, my church – and the world – had got on very well without me. I had known with my head that nobody is indispensable, but now I had experienced it. Major events, like earthquakes and floods had taken place, quite apart from all the minutiae of every-day family and church life. They had all happened without me. In fact some situations had positively flourished. The congregation seemed to have grown in my absence. This was very humbling and, at the same time, enormously encouraging. Again I had known with my head and given more than tacit assent to the 'priesthood of all believers' and the ministry of the 'whole people of God', but this was experiential learning.

In an unforgettable book Petru Dumitriu writes:

I shall not forget of what body I am such an infinitesimal part, nor in what direction we are oriented, pointed, directed; but without forgetting, for all that, to be humble, without thinking myself more than a grain of sand on the shore, a drop of water in the sea, a particle

of energy in the infinite universe, a tiny, a faint glimmer
soon to be fused with the absolute radiance of God.[3]

The book of Job also puts our all too human lives into
context:

> Where were you when I laid the foundation of the earth?
> Tell me, if you have understanding.
> Who determined its measurements – surely you know!
> Or who stretched the line upon it? (Job 38.4–5)

God has been around far longer than we mortals. What
passes for old in any antique shop cannot compare with the
'age' of God. In the words of Sydney Carter, 'you are older
than the world can be'.[4] I became slowly aware of the fact
that I know very little. In spite of a university education the
old adage rang bells: The more you know, the more you
realize you don't know. As Paul says, 'I regard everything
as loss because of the surpassing value of knowing Christ
Jesus my Lord' (Philemon 3.8).

Paul goes on to write about 'refuse', the rubbish which
he counts as worthless if it prevents him from gaining
Christ. Whatever life may be about, of one thing I am sure:
When we reach the end of our lives we are not going to be
asked what our golf handicap is, or who is top of the
Premier football division, or how much money we have, or
how many university degrees we have been awarded, or
how beautiful our garden is, but were we there when our
neighbour needed us. Not, let me hasten to add, that I am
a killjoy. I enjoy life and, indeed, enjoy many sports. It is
all a question of balance and, ultimately, if the purpose of
life is not to get close to God and to try to do his will, what
are we on earth for?

This brings me to the final and most important source of
assurance during the first week of prayer. I had the very
deep feeling that God wanted me to be on this retreat. Not
only that but since he desires nothing but my good then I

was, indeed, in good hands. When we say in our liturgy 'The Lord be with you' and respond with the words 'and also with you', how complacently we sometimes utter those words. But what powerful statements they are. God is with us always. Whether we are in pain, or rejoicing, at home relaxing, or at work, on our own or in company with others, God is with us.

Ignatius encourages retreatants to engage in what he calls a colloquy during the times of prayer. In other words to have a conversation with God about things that may be causing either consolation or desolation. One of my earliest conversations posed the question, 'Lord, how do I *know* you are there.' The reply came back almost immediately. 'I am, that's all you need to know.' It could be argued by an enquiring person that in prayerful colloquy I was simply talking to myself. This is very difficult to refute except to say that the experience felt different. When I am talking to myself the words come from my mouth. In this kind of prayer they come from elsewhere. Another Methodist minister did an eight-day retreat and experienced this and writes, 'there was an otherness about the replies which made me feel that I was engaged in a dialogue with him even when I heard him in my own voice'.[5]

The early meditations of the first week greatly helped to sensitize me to an awareness of the constant presence of God.

Do not fear, for I have redeemed you;
I have called you by your name, you are mine.
When you pass through the waters, I will be with you;
and through the rivers, they shall not overwhelm you;
 ... because you are precious in my sight. (Isaiah 43.1b–2a, 4a)

The Lord is gracious and merciful,
slow to anger and abounding in steadfast love.
The Lord is good to all,

and his compassion is over all that he has made. (Psalm
145.8–9)

Come to me, all you that are weary and are carrying
heavy burdens,
and I will give you rest.
Take my yoke upon you, and learn from me;
for I am gentle and humble in heart,
and you will find rest for your souls.
For my yoke is easy, and my burden is light. (Matthew
11.28–30)

We know that in everything God works for good
for those who love God,
who are called according to his purpose.
. . . for I am convinced that neither death, nor life..
nor anything else in all creation,
will be able to separate us from the love of God in Christ
Jesus our Lord. (Romans 8.28, 38a, 39b)

At this point my brain began to engage. It is all very well
to appreciate the constant presence of God but what about
the presence of evil in the world? We have all become
accustomed to the dreadful scenes of massacre in the war-
torn country that used to be called Yugoslavia. We have
seen the ravages of hunger producing emaciated faces and
pot-bellied children in the Horn of Africa. The work of
Amnesty International carries on unabated seeking the
release of prisoners of conscience in many parts of the
world. There are the evils of totalitarian states, of
homelessness, of racism, of sexual abuse. All over the
world there is an enormous amount of suffering. Where
does all this leave a God of love? 'The love of God should
work to counter the experience of Evil, just as prayer
should work to counter the evidence of the absence of
God.'[6] How can I engage in conversation with God when
there is so much evil and suffering in the world?

At the very least we have to acknowledge our own collusion with evil. This may well be through apathy, indifference, hatred, or simply lack of knowledge. We remain ignorant as to how our thirst for a higher standard of living in an age of consumerism robs people of their right to live in other parts of the world. Our problem is of eating too much, of wondering where to store all our food and often destroying mountains of it. Even as I went on one of my daily walks I was aware of a car pulling out in front of me. The exhaust fumes were considerable and this from just one car. There is pressure to build another terminal at Heathrow, near to where I used to live. Is there any thought given to the quality of the lives of people in the neighbourhood already breathing pollution and coping with intense levels of noise? Are we slowly poisoning ourselves with smoke, tobacco, drugs and alcohol? No discussion of evil and suffering can take place without acknowledging our steadfast reluctance to become involved in issues of peace and justice. We have allowed our Christianity to become privatized. Our prayer is in danger of becoming a personal dialogue between me and my Maker omitting the needs of our neighbour.

When we look at the problems of injustice, of world hunger, of homelessness, violence, the arms trade, the threat of nuclear defence systems to human existence, we can feel overwhelmed by the enormity of the problems and our helplessness to effect any change. We need to stay with our helplessness until we realize that we are leaving God out, 'who by the power at work within us is able to accomplish abundantly far more than all we can ask or imagine' (Ephesians 3.20).[7]

During this first week of prayer I firmly resisted my own feelings of sin. After all I felt I led a reasonably good life. To be sure not a perfect life, but nevertheless I did try to get involved with peace and justice issues. I had written to my

MP recently about a number of local and national issues. I try to exercise a pastoral ministry especially to those in greatest need: the ill, the bereaved, the suffering. Furthermore I have been conscious in my ministry of travelling by faith. There have been many instances where that faith has sustained me. I have cried out with Peter, 'Lord, save me!' (Matthew 14.30). What did I need to confess? 'If we say we have no sin, we deceive ourselves, and the truth is not in us' (1 John 1.8). Where was I deceiving myself?

Superficially one can bemoan the state of one's life in terms of one's particular weaknesses. Perhaps you are overweight, or you refuse to take any exercise, or you overindulge when you go shopping, or you spend a lot of time on yourself and your own needs, or you are a workaholic, or you succumb too readily to any form of temptation. The list of weaknesses can be endless. However, at a deeper level when one focuses on the spiritual life, weaknesses can certainly be found there. How much time do we spend in prayer, or quiet meditation before God? How often do we focus on our own autonomy and independence? Surely, we imply, we can get on very well without God. We can invest a great deal of pride in our own abilities.

God has blessed me with a capacity to think and therefore it seemed right to be ever ready to engage my critical faculties in searching for the truth, especially in biblical texts. This has been part of my theological training. There will be more to say about this in Chapter 5. For the moment let me say that perhaps I had concentrated too much on my doubts and on my own capacities and did not have enough trust in God. Faith has most definitely been part of my life and this does allow for the presence of doubt because faith is not the accumulation of our certainties, otherwise it would not be faith. However the word that sprang to mind was trust or rather my lack of it. Concentrating on my own abilities and capacities was not a demonstration of trust. In the words of John the Baptist when he says of Jesus, 'He must increase, but I must decrease' (John 3.30).

A meditation during this first week was on the parable of the Prodigal Son (Luke 15.11–32). This has always been my favourite parable. I have preached on it many times. It is a wonderful expression of the forgiveness of God. There is the remarkable picture of the aged father actually looking out for his son and then running to meet him, and embracing him and giving him symbols of acceptance and authority, not to mention a party. He gives all of this to someone who had lived with gentiles and eaten with pigs which to Jews are unclean animals. Here really was a lost son. The Jews would have given up on him. Yet the father goes out to meet him and kisses him. He also goes out to the elders who apparently has missed the party and complains that 'I never disobeyed your command'. Thereby the elder son is identified with the Pharisees. This is a parable about two sons who were lost and the father forgives them both.

All of the above is true at one level, the level of biblical interpretation. However, for the first time I entered this parable at a different level. What does the text actually mean to me? Where am I in it? Who or what do I identify with? To my great surprise I found myself identifying with the prodigal son. This was a surprise because I did not feel as though I was in exile, nor had I squandered my property in loose living and I certainly had not been in such a desperate position of wanting to eat the food that pigs were eating. Where was the identification coming from? The key verse was 'how many of my father's hired hands have bread enough and to spare, but here I am dying of hunger!' I began to see myself as spiritually starving. I had certainly felt dissatisfied with my own prayer life and lack of it for some time. Had I been satisfied in eating spiritual 'pods' when all the time there was bread to eat? The significance and symbolism of bread in the New Testament need not be elaborated on here. I made the decision there and then to go back to my Father and before I knew it he came running to meet me! This was quite overwhelming. Oh, yes! I had preached about forgiveness till I was blue in the face, but now I experienced it at a very deep level for the very first time.

Perchance to dream

It should not be thought that all the changes took place at the level of conscious thought or through the awareness of my feelings and emotions. Due to the heightened level of awareness I often had very vivid dreams. Normally I find it difficult to recall my dreams, indeed I am not usually conscious of having dreamt at all. However, on retreat, there is not the same daily 'busyness'. There is more time for reflection and this leads to a greater degree of sensitivity and general awareness of what God is saying not only through the conscious side of our lives but also through the unconscious side. I remembered Freud's well-known dictum that dreams are the royal road to the unconscious.

On one occasion I was taking my sons and daughter to look round my old school. I was very disconcerted to discover that I could not find the way. I had to ask someone where it was.

A similar theme occurred in a dream when I found myself on the golf links where I used to play as a small child. To my amazement the golf links no longer existed. They had been built on. I felt I had to go and tell my mother. On the way home I became completely lost. Nothing was the same as it used to be. I remember asking someone the way and they could not understand how I could be so lost. Eventually through all the buildings and the maze of streets my eyes lighted upon a church. Then I knew where I was. I had found my bearings again. I could find my way home from there.

There was another occasion when I dreamt about

moving house. It was a good-looking house but a bit decrepit. I remember taking down the curtains, cleaning up the place and handing over the keys. There was great excitement. The trouble was I did not know where I was moving to. The dream was all about moving out, not moving in.

In another dream I found myself playing the organ. I was happily playing a hymn tune to which everyone was singing and then I began to play some wrong notes. I looked at the music. It wasn't there! There was a strong feeling of panic. At the best of times I find it difficult to play anything without music even if the piece is very well known. When I awoke my interpretation of this dream was that in my ministry I had been playing some wrong notes. In fact I had been using the wrong music. I had been playing with the head and not the heart. Now I was learning to play and to listen with the heart. Quite literally I found this to be mind-blowing. We shall return to this theme in Chapter 7.

These and many other dreams were very much part of my retreat. Clearly a psychoanalyst would have a wonderful time trying to interpret them. The message that came through to me was that things were changing inside. Internal structures, which I had felt comfortable with and with which I was familiar, were beginning to change. My foundations were being shaken. Some of the symbols seem to refer to a way of thinking, cerebral processes. Now it seems I was being asked to use a different mode of understanding. On one occasion I went for a walk and the countryside was covered in snow. The external appearance was quite different although underneath things were just the same. The reverse was true for me. The outer appearance was just the same but underneath a radical change had taken place.

But we must come back from the Land of Nod to reality. I was beginning to experience sin at an ever-deeper level. There seemed no end to the torrid time I was having.

Experiencing sin

I thought about some of the things I had said that I wish I hadn't said and my hesitation in saying things that I could have said. The right words always seem to come after the event, when it is too late. Why can't I think of the right words at the right time? I meditated on the parable of the Rich Fool (Luke 12.16–21). This is the story of the man who wanted to build bigger and better barns and said to himself,

'Soul, you have ample goods laid up for many years; relax, eat, drink, be merry.' But God said to him, 'You fool! This night your life is being demanded of you. And the things you have prepared, whose will they be?'

I have always sat lightly to material possessions, but didn't I resent never having enough money? The ministry is not the place to be if you want to acquire wealth. Far from it. If only I had become a clinical psychologist then I would have had enough and to spare. You fool! You have always had enough and to spare. What more do you want? Didn't I always want a house of my own to live in? Wasn't I always looking at other people's houses and feeling somewhat jealous? You fool. What are you worrying about? You have a beautiful house to live in.

Have I got things right in my ministry? You are involved in a life of doing rather than being. You have become more like a social worker. You fool. What are you offering people? Not even a full barn, more like an empty one. What about your church? It has been doing all the right things but it is like a car trying to run on the wrong petrol. It will go places but only very slowly and with a lot of pushing. You fool. What about prayer? You have been living on your past stores. You have been taking your ease; eating, drinking and being merry. There is a great sense of urgency in this parable. This night your soul is required of you. Not next week, or next year, not when we feel ready, not in our time but in God's time. Paul sums up the sense of frustration precisely. 'I can will what is right, but I cannot do it. For I do not do the good I want, but the evil I do not want is what I do. Now if I do what I do not want, it is no longer I that do it, but sin which dwells within me' (Romans 7.18b–20).

I began to feel a great need of some inner cleansing. An outward sign of this was that I drank far less coffee and just drank water. I also began to eat less. No longer did I eat puddings or chocolate. I even had a great desire to clean up my kitchen and bedroom. This was not because they were particularly dirty. It was an inner drive for cleanliness. The great penitential psalm puts it thus, 'Wash me thoroughly from my iniquity, and cleanse me from my sin!' (Psalm 51.2).

It seems so utterly selfish to think about our petty wants and desires, to focus on ourselves instead of on the needs of other people. Particularly is this true when we see ourselves in the light of the cross. Again to use the words of Paul, 'But God proves his love for us in that while we were yet sinners Christ died for us' (Romans 5.8). As we say in the communion service, 'This is my body given for you, this is my blood poured out for you.'

Another dream depicted a funeral taking place. The mourners had placed a cross on the coffin but when the funeral service took place the cross was not there. This provoked great consternation among those present. The power of the cross began to be felt at this stage but the full force of it became even more apparent during the third week.

Wrestling with God

Towards the end of this first phase of the Exercises I began to feel a sense of anger welling up inside me. The reasons for this are not relevant, but I felt angry with God. It seemed to me that in part of my life he had let me down. I wanted some straight answers. Before a particular session of prayer I prepared myself for battle. I was not even going to use any biblical verses, nothing that would in any way prove to be a distraction. In order to make this a fair fight with God I removed the large crucifix which was an aid to devotion during this first week, and the cushion on which it was placed and a small plant which was also in view. I did however light the candle. There I was, with God. Just the two of us.

I began this hour of prayer by kneeling. God spoke. 'All you have to do is listen.' I refused point blank. I folded my arms in a gesture of defensive defiance. I was not going to listen. I looked for all sorts of distractions mental and physical. Eventually I felt impelled to open my arms. I heard a voice. 'There is no need to kneel, just sit, relax and listen. The first thing you have to do is to put the crucifix back.' I refused. Again there was the gesture of defiance; the folded arms. This was a wrestling match to end all wrestling matches. I was not going to be bullied by God. After a long, long interval of time, I weakened. First the cushion went back, and then the crucifix and then the plant. 'No, don't put the plant at the side, put it at the foot of the cross.' There it was in a nutshell. Life was at the foot of the cross. I found this to be quite overwhelming and totally unexpected. If I had thought about this beforehand would I have come to this conclusion? Would I have worked it out like this? I think not. This was a wonderful acting out of the mystery of the cross. This symbol of suffering which stretches across the centuries as a beacon of light in a dark world. What a mystery and paradox the cross is.

'But what about my anger, the reason for my anger?'

'Just leave it to me', was the reply. As with most of the examples I am writing about their initial impact is lost as soon as they are committed to paper. Indeed, they almost appear to be trite. This was most certainly not the case at the time. Suffice it to say that I finished this session in a state of shock, but God had not finished with me.

On fasting

In the first week there began to be two kinds of feelings that could be broadly categorized as those which took me deeper into God and those that did not. The spiritual life is a constant process of discernment, deciding which processes are of God and those which are not. God is always drawing us to himself, towards a life of greater faith, hope, love and trust. The movement of the Holy Spirit tends towards attraction, peacefulness and gentleness. Thus, if we are greatly troubled, the chances are that this is not a movement of the Holy Spirit. On these occasions we usually feel at loggerheads within ourselves or, to use another image, we have a stone heart instead of a heart of flesh (Ezekiel 36.26).

A movement of destruction came as I focused on the cross and uttered the cry of derision, 'if you are the Son of God, come down from the cross and save yourself'. The cross was too powerful; I could not look at it. This cry was a defence. Save yourself, not me. My stubbornness was not going to let God in. Then I would begin to lose control and anything might happen. 'My heart is stricken and withered like grass; I am too waisted to eat my bread . . . for I eat ashes like bread, and mingle tears with my drink' (Psalm 102.4, 9). The powerful imagery of this psalm, the stupidity of eating ashes rather than bread, eventually moved me to look at the cross. I listened again. 'I have been there, I will save you.'

This was a week of great struggle, of oppression, of inner battles and torment. Just as I was beginning to experience a deep sense of peace at having passed through 'the refiner's fire' and survived, just as I was aching for a period in which to cool off, a thunderbolt hit me.

I was praying in the chapel. There were sisters from the community also praying. The atmosphere was one of great peace and tranquillity. I reflected on Romans 12.14–21. In particular verse 16, 'Live in harmony with one another', rang bells. Feeling very much at peace after the troubles and torments of the previous few days I conjured up all sorts of images of peace and harmony, sitting in the garden on a summer's day, or wallowing in the sun on a tropical beach. A glance outside gave the impression that even the world seemed to have stopped. There was the vision of a new heaven and a new earth where there would be no more pain, no suffering and no tears. All was silent and at peace, within and without.

Suddenly, a searing shudder went through me. Where did it come from? I remembered deep within my being some occasions, long since repressed, when I had not lived in harmony with my fellow brothers and sisters. Indeed when there was, or could have been, the possibility of complete discord and disaster. There was a great feeling of agitation and physical sickness. I left the chapel in great distress with an intense desire to eliminate something from my body. This was not because of something I had eaten but because of a great psycho-spiritual need. A purging process was needed.

We fool ourselves into thinking an action is right when it is clearly wrong. We entertain a highly selective memory in that we recall only those experiences that we want to and it is usually the pleasant ones. Psychoanalytic studies have clearly shown us how we use defence mechanisms, unconsciously, to protect our psyche from all that would be too difficult or painful to bear. On this retreat my defences were gradually being stripped away. I felt myself naked before God. This was a very chastening experience. Tears were plentiful. The tears were part of the process of purification. 'Let us approach with a true heart in full assurance of faith, with our hearts sprinkled clean from an evil conscience and our bodies washed with pure water' (Hebrews 10.22).

As a result of this morning of drama and tension I was absolutely ravenous. However, for the first time in my life I felt the need to fast. On this occasion eating lunch would have been wrong. An immense surge of energy welled up within me and I went for a long, long walk, in the rain and driving wind. I know not where the energy came from or where I walked. It did not matter. I was only aware that what on an earlier occasion had appeared to be a huge field with green shoots was now perceived as a green field.

Now I know what spiritual fasting is not. It is not the desire to lose weight. It is not refusing to eat because you do not feel hungry. It is not because it feels like a good idea or because it tells you to do so in the Bible or because you are being sponsored for some charitable cause. It is not even doing without something because then you might feel less guilty about having so much when others have so little. It is not about eating less so that you can more fully empathize with those who regularly eat very little or nothing at all. Fasting may include some or all of the above. However, fasting essentially is a spiritual desire coming from deep within. It is a hunger, a thirst, and a desire to purge yourself and thus be closer to God. For this to happen, food is no longer important except as a means for maintaining life.

All of this may seem very dramatic and even unreal. Let me assure those who have read so far that this experience was far more dramatic and real when I actually experienced it. The final act centred on Psalm 130. This was the meditation that had been set aside for me on returning from this long walk in the rain after almost literally being driven out of the convent chapel by my inner anguish. This is a psalm about waiting for the Lord. Not as a watchman waits for the dawn because he knows when the dawn is coming and it is a very passive waiting. Waiting for the Lord is far more active. 'I wait for the Lord, my soul waits, and in his word I hope' (verse 5). Moreover we never know at what point the Lord is ready to break into our experience or in what way he will break in. God is a God of surprises. Indeed a best-seller has been written on this very theme as a result of the author having undergone these Spiritual Exercises.[8]

However, on this occasion the main impact of the psalm hit home like an arrow splitting an apple. 'If thou, O Lord, should mark iniquities, Lord, who could stand? . . . But there is forgiveness with you, so that you may be revered.' For with the Lord there is steadfast love, and with him is great power to redeem (verses 3, 4 and 7b). What more needs to be said? Perhaps for the first time in my life I felt totally and completely at peace.

As a postscript to this meditation I noticed in the burning candle before me that a small piece of wax was constantly drawn into the flame and would then suddenly dart out again to the periphery. There is a tendency in the Christian life to flirt with God. That is, we get glimpses as to what the kingdom may be all about and then, because, as it were, the heat is too great, we dash to the edges. My understanding is that true peace, and true understanding, is only found if we constantly try to dwell at the centre of the flame, in the heart of God.

After 25 years in the Methodist ministry I had made the startling discovery that I was a beginner in the spiritual life. But what is spirituality?

4

The search for spirituality

During the whole of my ministry the membership of the church in Britain has declined. It comes as a slight relief to know that this decline started long before I was born. W.E. Sangster wrote a book about it called *Methodism Can Be Born Again*.[1] This was written in 1938 and in it he asks the question, 'Why are people leaving the Church?' Some of the answers Sangster gives seem surprisingly contemporary. 'Dull services, irrelevant preaching and a loss of power in prayer' are mentioned.[2] He cites 'counter attractions' on Sundays:

> The cinema is enticingly open on Sunday evening ... hiking and cycling prove seductive to thousands of young people. Even the motor-car must bear its part of the blame ... How much the wireless has affected church attendance it is not easy to say ... some seem to have proposed this question to themselves: 'Why drag to church to hear poor preaching, when you can sit comfortably at home, and hear it done well on the air?'[3]

As I said these reasons have a surprising contemporary ring. Of course we could add a host of extra attractions in which people participate today on Sundays. This, though, is not the place for such an analysis. Other people have recently written on the issue from different standpoints. Rob Frost writes, 'the haemorrhaging of church life has continued unabated while the traditional denominations have been paralysed to respond'.[4] Leslie Richter and Philip

Francis write that one of the reasons people leave churches is so that they can grow.[5] People often seem to outgrow their church and leaving it is a necessary part of growing up.

Whatever reasons we give for the decline in church membership, however we seek to analyze the statistics, it does seem to me that there is no corresponding lack of interest in spirituality. Some evidence for this came at the time of the sudden death of Diana, Princess of Wales. Huge numbers of people had a burning desire to express their grief by placing flowers at the gates of Kensington Palace. There seemed to be a need to express the inexpressible, a need to make an exterior manifestation of the interior shock and grief. People were faced with their own mortality and the need to answer the question 'What is life all about?' especially when such a popular icon of beauty could die in so untimely a way. Furthermore whenever there is a tragedy, for example a road traffic accident, people often express their grief by forming an impromptu shrine and possibly lighting a candle. More evidence comes for the presence of spirituality from parents who want their baby baptized but rarely, if ever, darken the doors of a church. They confess to believing in God and certainly feel it is right for their baby to be received into God's loving purposes, but the church, quite frankly, is seen to be irrelevant to their everyday life. People also talk about, and take part in, pilgrimages. There has recently been an exhibition at the National Gallery depicting the various ways in which artists through the century have depicted Jesus. Each day the exhibition has been packed with people. It has been one of the most successful millennium exhibitions.

This kind of evidence although important can really only be described as anecdotal but it does show that people have more than a modicum of spirituality within themselves. The search for a spiritual meaning to life is also exemplified in a recent novel.[6] A more scientific approach comes from the oft-quoted research of David Hay.[7] 'Surveys show that probably two thirds of the population feel that they have a spiritual dimension to their existence ... based on their practical experience of life.'[8] Hay claims that two thirds of adults have a personal spirituality, but fewer than one in ten people bother to go to church.[9]

Clearly a distinction is being made between religion and spirituality. The former is concerned with institutions, rites and rituals. It is about one of the formal religions of the world. The latter is much harder to define. Simon Bailey gives an enigmatic story about a holy woman who always sits on a box. The villagers are curious to know what is in the box. When she says it is a secret they are even more curious. Finally she opens the lid and the box is empty. 'Grumbling and complaining and puzzled, the villagers drifted away. But a few remained. The saint sat down on the ground with the silent villagers around the open box and together they contemplated the Secret of the Box.'[10]

Defining spirituality is, clearly, no easy matter. However it would be too vague to say that spirituality is whatever we decide to put in 'the box' but it would certainly include material and research from history, anthropology, sociology, psychology and literature. Perhaps more helpfully spirituality has been defined as:

> a quality that goes beyond religious affiliation, that strives for inspiration, awe, meaning and purpose, even in those who do not believe in any god. The spiritual dimension tries to be in harmony with the universe, strives for answers about the infinite and comes into focus when a person faces emotional stress, physical illness and death.[11]

It is about the search for meaning and purpose in life, the search for wholeness and for authentic existence. Spirituality acknowledges there is more to life than the things we see. Note that spirituality 'goes beyond religious affiliation'. Indeed spirituality is increasingly disassociated from clearly defined religious belief systems. This postmodern world is a world of options and preferences rather than a world of 'givens'. Spirituality is something that is freely chosen rather than inherited. The only 'given' is the existence of God.

One of the problems is that religion, rather than fostering and nurturing people's hunger for spirituality, sometimes extinguishes it. People can become so involved in maintaining the religious structures and their particular traditions and buildings that the deeper questions of life are not faced. This maintenance has involved the holding of bazaars, jumble sales and other money-raising events which are a far cry from any issues relating to spirituality. All too often in the church we have been more concerned with maintenance and doing things in what are perceived to be the right ways.

Recently I saw a vintage car. It was in pristine condition, absolutely immaculate. Under the bonnet was a sight to behold. There was not a trace of oil, dirt or grime. The whole engine gleamed and shone. I couldn't but think of the effort and time put into this car which was now no longer needed except as a period piece. Most of the year was spent under wraps. Is this what happens to the church? A vast amount of time and effort is spent on keeping it in good condition but the reality is that people find it irrelevant? It no longer meets their everyday needs.

We have been eager to provide the answers instead of engaging with the world to discover what the questions are. We have been guilty of providing the medicine when we have not bothered to find out what the illness is.

Formal religion with its trappings and power games, is proving to be a major obstacle to spiritual growth and development. Religion sets limitations, and lures the seeker into dealing with issues which seem to belong to the perpetuation of the system rather than the growth of the person.[12]

Someone rather cynically has said, 'hands off the church, it is the one thing that can keep us from Christianity'.[13] One might also add that the church could be the thing that prevents people facing the basic questions of life.

The worst excesses of these 'power games' can be seen in religious fundamentalism. In a rapidly changing world there is a desire not only to know but to be absolutely certain. Things are either black or white and there are no shades of grey. Psychologically this is called an 'intolerance of ambiguity' and is dealt with in the textbooks. Robert Towler has studied the phenomenon from a sociological point of view.[14] Certitude is the absence of doubt and the need for certitude is the attempt to escape from doubt. Such certitude is not what faith is about. Indeed it is the very opposite of faith. Faith is not the sum total of our certainties, nor is it about avoiding all doubt.

> If one knows something with complete certainty, then, by definition, what is thus certainly known cannot be transcendent. That which is beyond one can only be aspired to and reached toward, never grasped. Certitude is a stunted growth compared with faith.[15]

The ecumenical endeavour

It is one short step from acknowledging that we are in the right and God is on our side to saying that everybody else is wrong. This automatically brings to an end any constructive dialogue between other faiths or, indeed, between other denominations. As long as Methodists, for example, subconsciously believe that God is a Methodist there is no chance of the ecumenical endeavour surviving let alone prospering. We can become so committed to our way of doing things that it is taken for granted that it is the right way of doing things.

Much of the energy of clergy and parishioners can be

expended on trivial changes, draining everyone of the energy required to love and to serve. That is why those who pride themselves on being the most loyal, committed and orthodox may also be the most Christless in their attitude to those who disagree with them.[16]

Sixty years ago Sangster wrote, 'nothing seems clearer about the religious mood of the present time than that denominationalism is out of favour. Hardly anyone can be discovered who will defend the sectarian spirit.'[17] Happily, since then there have been some small steps forward but the ecumenical endeavour will not really succeed while it remains low on the agenda of churches. While churches are so preoccupied with their own survival there is simply not enough surplus energy to expend on issues which involve working with other denominations. There has to be a basic desire to be obedient to what God is demanding of us. That will undoubtedly mean letting go of some of our long-cherished customs and beliefs. It will also mean waiting on God in prayer to discover where God is leading us and what he is demanding of us. There is no blue-print for ecumenism and movements towards church unity will be more effective if they come from the grass roots. Whatever is imposed from above will not work unless there is a desire among congregations to build up love and trust.

Church unity is not about a take-over bid by one Church of all the other Churches, but about listening to one another across the denominations, working together in obedience to the Spirit, the Spirit of unity and of peace poured out on all peoples.[18]

Religious schizophrenia

Spirituality is about being more open, more willing to listen rather than provide the answers. It is finding God in everyone, for Jesus is 'the true light which, enlightens everyone' (John 1.9). Precisely because we find God in the other person, precisely because God is already in the world, spirituality can never be seen as an exercise in individual narcissism. True spirituality always brings with it a concern for issues of peace and justice. Of course in all of us there can be a tendency towards a sort of spiritual schizophrenia, Hyde on Sunday and Jekyll on Monday. This religious split is noticeable when we consider some of the radical demands of the Sermon on the Mount and the way that most of us live our lives. Gerard Hughes gives a superb example of this when he talks about nuclear deterrence.[19]

In another place Hughes writes:

> our spirituality is so split that most Christians believe that world hunger, homelessness, the arms trade, war itself, are political questions, not religious and therefore unsuitable topics for the pulpit. Such a split personality is attractive to the better off. It was attractive to Dives and enabled him to dine sumptuously everyday, without even noticing Lazarus.[20]

Jesus railed against this religious split in the Pharisees who did not practise what they preached (Matthew 23.1–5). He also chided the disciples for arguing amongst themselves as to who was the greatest (Luke 22.24–27). It is a very typical human response to argue about who has the authority, who has the control, who has the power, but the irony is that the discussion comes immediately after the comradeship of the Last Supper.

One of the aims of the Spiritual Exercises of Ignatius is to see God in all things and thus avoid dividing the world into sacred and secular. In a profound sense all the world is sacred. If we could be more aware we would see that every bush is burning. We would certainly see that God is not just in church on Sundays. He is actually in the world wherever we happen to find ourselves on Monday morning.

There is nothing God has made that cannot be used to speak to us of God and to lead us to God; if we want to explore the length and breadth, the depth and height of God's love, then we must look all around us, for creation is full of it.[21]

The Jesuit poet Gerard Manley Hopkins wrote, 'the world is charged with the grandeur of God'. All of life, the created world *and* human experience exhibits the power of the Creator. If only we could see!

The angels keep their ancient places –
Turn but a stone, and start a wing!
'Tis ye, 'tis your estranged faces,
That miss the many-splendour'd thing.[22]

One of the reasons for our blindness is that we are caught up in ourselves. Recently I missed the opportunity to share a beautiful sunset with my wife because I wanted to boil some plums! We become slaves to our passions and selfish desires. There are pressures to succeed and to be seen to be succeeding. There are demands for our time, money and attention. We are persuaded to buy things that we don't need and to do things that are not life-giving. Most of us are preoccupied with the demands of everyday living: the endless round of paying bills and making ends meet, bringing up children, facing unemployment or redundancy, making sure that the latest work appraisal scheme shows you are up to scratch, ensuring that elderly parents are cared for and so on, and so on. The list is endless. However Ignatian spirituality does not suggest that God can only be found during periods of heightened concentration, for example, during a retreat. Far from it. Ignatius, in his First Principle and Foundation categorically states that:

the other things on the face of the earth are created for the human beings, to help them in working toward the end for which they are created. From this it follows that I should use these things to the extent that they help me toward my end, and rid myself of them to the extent that they hinder me.[23]

All of life is created by God including the things that happen to us. We deny God when we deny our experience. Where is God in this thing that is happening to me? Where is God in the person sitting next to me on the bus? In the daily headlines? In the family argument? In the terminal cancer? In the decision to be made? In the Bible passage? In the family party? In the church meeting? What is God saying to me in all these situations? Sometimes the answer may be obvious, but at other times it needs to be prayed about and thought about. In fact it is precisely when the going gets rough and we have to work hard at the question of what God is saying that we move on in the spiritual life. When everything in the garden is rosy we tend to remain static and don't even ask the relevant questions. Paul affirms that 'all things work together for good'(Romans 8.28), but only for 'those who love God'. God speaks to us through all our experience but only if we are receptive to him.

From a completely different but more contemporary standpoint, the psychotherapist Carl Rogers argues for the importance of listening to experience. '*I can trust my experience . . . experience is, for me, the highest authority*' (his italics). The touchstone of validity is my own experience. No other person's ideas, and none of my own ideas, are as authoritative as my experience. It is to experience that I must return again and again.[24] For Rogers this experience is about getting in touch with his own feelings. 'When an activity feels as though it is valuable or worth doing, it *is* worth doing'.[25] Rogers goes on to talk about hunches or vague thoughts that feel as though they are significant. This totality of experience is reckoned to be wiser than the intellect.

5

Facts and feelings

Now, what I want is, Facts. Teach these boys and girls nothing but Facts. Facts alone are wanted in life. Plant nothing else, and root out everything else. You can only form the minds of reasoning animals upon Facts: nothing else will ever be of service to them. This is the principle on which I bring up my own children, and this is the principle on which I bring up these children. Stick to Facts, Sir! In this life, we want nothing but Facts, Sir; nothing but Facts![1]

This was the guiding principle for Mr Thomas Gradgrind as he carried out his duties as a schoolteacher. Such an approach completely floored one of his pupils when she was asked to define a horse. She obviously knew what a horse was since her father was a horse-breaker. However she was unable to define and give a precise description of something which to her was quite obvious. A boy in the class gave an answer which seemed to satisfy Mr Gradgrind:

Quadruped. Graminivorous. Forty teeth, namely twenty-five grinders, four eyeteeth, and twelve incisive. Sheds coat in the Spring; in marshy countries, sheds hoofs, too. Hoofs hard, but requiring to be shod with iron. Age known by marks in mouth.[2]

This is certainly one level of communication. What the girl thought of the definition we shall never know. After all she knew quite well what a horse was from her own experience. In prayer we are using another mode of communication which is based on trust. We converse with God in our hearts. Gerard Hughes gives the example of a child being frightened of the dark. Mother picks the child up and says, 'It's all right' and the child hopefully drops off to sleep. If, however her child is akin to the boy in Mr Gradgrind's class he might say to his mother, 'What epistemological and metaphysical assumptions are you making in that statement, and what empirical evidence can you adduce in support of your contention?'[3] If this is the case, the head has taken over and the trust has gone.

Clearly, during this retreat, I was following the promptings of my heart. However, as we have seen, numerous questions were often asked about the text. Indeed to follow those promptings poses a question in itself. I was constantly aware of this tension and conflict within myself. In this chapter we shall try to discover if and how the two approaches can be reconciled. Is belief a matter for the head or for the heart?

Thinking

Our education system is designed to promote not only the accumulation of facts and the passing of examinations but the ability to engage in critical thought. The same is true of theological colleges. Certainly when I was studying for the ministry the approach was what can be described as critical. In other words it was an approach of enquiry. Questions about the authorship of the various books of the Bible were asked. When were they written and who for? Do the records give a picture of Jesus as divine or human? What is the meaning, for example, of the title 'Son of Man'? What was the meaning of the original Greek or Hebrew? These questions are quite properly the domain of biblical criticism and historical analysis. This is an approach that uses the left side of the brain. This is the cerebral hemisphere that uses language and works things out by logical analysis. Its function can be described as linear, systematic thinking.

Education is a process that is almost totally dominated by the need to improve this kind of thinking. The notable French psychologist Piaget constructed a theory of child development with which all schoolteachers are familiar. The final stage of his theory is called the stage of 'formal operations' and is closely associated with book learning. In this stage the adolescent is able to engage in systematic thinking. Theories can be formulated and tested. It is the ability to conceive of possibilities which are beyond the present reality; to be concerned with ideological and philosophical problems. There is a questioning approach to everything. In formal operational thinking the mind takes off. Erikson and Kohlberg have also constructed theories of human development, the latter's work being an extension of Piaget's theory to the area of moral development. A central thrust of Kohlberg's work is that moral judgment and action have a rational core.

James Fowler has used the work of Piaget to devise a theory of religious development.[4] He also postulates that there are stages in development. Stage 3 is called 'synthetic conventional faith' and is characterized, as in the case of the formal operations stage of cognitive development, by a keen interest in questions and ideas and thinking for its own sake. Having been a university chaplain for 11 years I can testify to the veracity of this stage. Students love to engage in endless discussions till the early hours about 'the meaning of life, the universe and everything'. There are other characteristics but this is not the place for a detailed discussion.

Stage 4 is called 'individuative-reflective faith'. Here the individual begins to challenge beliefs and value systems. This is a time of critical reflection. 'Always be ready to make your defence to any one who demands from you an account of the hope that is in you' (1 Peter 3.15). Beliefs which were previously tacit and unexamined convictions are now put under the microscope and either defended or discarded. It needs to be said that this stage of critical examination is not easy. For many it is perceived to be too much of a challenge to their faith. They are more concerned with hanging on to certainties rather than accommodating doubts.

Stage 5 is the stage of 'conjunctive faith'. Here the individual is more able to live and tolerate ambiguity. There is an awareness of the

> need to face and hold together several unmistakable polar tensions in one's life; the polarities of being both old and young and of being both masculine and feminine. Further, it means integrating the polarity of being both constructive and destructive and the polarity of having both a conscious and a shadow self.[5]

In other words, the person learns to live with paradoxes and contradictions. For example, how can God be a God of love when there is so much evil in the world?

Of paramount importance here is the fact that in stage 5 the person is more able to cope with beliefs that contradict logical testing and is more inclined to look for truth and meaning in the deeper aspects of the self. In other words, truth can be found at a variety of different levels. The cognitive level is only one. Fowler himself uses an illustration from science. Light can be explained either by the wave theory or the particle theory; a wave phenomenon or particles of energy. Each of this provides only a partial explanation of the characteristics of light. Both are needed.

Whether these stages are a progression is a moot point and, however the transition between various stages takes place, the issue here is that in stage 5 there is a realization that there are at least two levels of truth. In terms of religious faith this means that we can apprehend the images of Christianity through thought, the cognitive processes, or through the emotions and the deeper levels of the unconscious. It is this latter level which the Ignatian approach emphasizes. Instead of analyzing a biblical text and extracting its meaning by critical exegesis, in Ignatian prayer one has to learn how to let the text do the work of bringing one's needs and feelings to the level of consciousness.

Beginning to feel

The problem here is that we live in a culture which underestimates feelings. We are more concerned with facts and the processes of logical thought. This is more of a problem for men. 'Little boys don't cry'; 'Don't be such a wimp.' This is the tyranny of the stiff upper lip. It was not until I was in my mid-twenties and embarked upon a course of counselling that I really knew how to answer the question, 'How do you feel?' Hitherto I had studied at three universities and therefore had been preoccupied with facts and thoughts. Most of the time I actually didn't know how I felt. It was an irrelevance. I knew what I thought but not what I felt.

Feelings are neither good nor bad. They just are. How we articulate them and give vent to them is quite another matter. However the first step is to acknowledge that we have feelings. We may not be able to name them, let alone express them, but we all have them.

The Christian life often remains at the level of superficiality because we find it hard to express our feelings. Fellowship can be phoney and artificial if we are not honest with each other. Our feelings are the things that really matter. All the philosophical tomes about the existence of God, all the theological statements about the resurrection, the truth of Genesis, or the exegesis of a particular biblical verse are all words, empty vacuous words, if we do not love our neighbour. 'If I speak in the tongues of mortals and angels, but do not have love, I am a noisy gong or a clanging cymbal' (1 Corinthians 13.1). Love does not mean bombarding with words or abstract arguments, love means listening. Listening attentively, actively, empathetically as another person expresses their feelings is a profound act of love and therefore of inestimable value. Listening really takes on a new dimension when we listen with our eyes. When we are not being distracted by other sights and sounds, but visibly demonstrating that we are giving the speaker our undivided attention.

Although the Christian philosophy of life is based upon love there is nevertheless a prevailing attitude that the expression of feelings can be destructive. People often find it more acceptable to be 'nice' to each other. This is usually at the cost of honesty. We can find our integrity swallowed up in our desire to project a friendly face and a desire to be considered acceptable by the other person. The very real danger is that, if we employ this approach, the irritation, frustration, anger, or whatever the unexpressed feeling is, can then come out sideways rather than being directed at the person who is arousing the feeling. It can very quickly get into the area of malicious gossip, heavy sarcasm or sheer bad temper. Even if that does not happen the thought itself can produce as much guilt as if the deed had actually been carried out.

An example of how feelings can come out sideways is when, at a church meeting, Mr Reliable suddenly announces his resignation from a position of responsibility within the congregation. This decision comes right out of the blue without any prior warning and seems, moreover, to be completely without rhyme or reason. Indeed, in later conversation Mr Reliable vehemently denies that anything in particular was the cause of his resignation. He makes up some highly plausible reason like pressing family or work commitments. However, it subsequently transpires as a result of some judicious probing that the cause of the action was no such thing. Somebody, and it is often the minister, had said or done something of which he had strongly disapproved. The anger had been repressed and so it had surfaced quite unexpectedly. A more helpful and liberating course of action would have been to talk to the instigator of the anger in an atmosphere of Christian love and forgiveness and thus brought the matter into the light of day. (This is what Lord Soper called the 'fellowship of controversy'.) In this way both parties would have grown. How can the third party do anything to repair the damage if it does not know what it has done?

Another way in which the feelings can come out is via the family. Sometimes in the face of a seemingly innocuous and harmless remark or action the children 'get their heads bitten off' and they wonder what on earth they have done to warrant such treatment. They are subdued with the comment 'Dad is in a bad mood' or 'Mum is tired'. The bad mood and the tiredness often result from bending over backwards to accommodate people and put them in the best possible light while the self hurriedly backs away, retreats, and somehow loses its essential honesty and integrity. A cardboard, overadjusted personality is left which simply agrees with everyone.

Nor is it just a loss of integrity. Somehow the person's own feelings are totally ignored in deference to the other person. This has its dangers. Anthony Storr puts it thus, 'to identify with another person is to lose oneself, to submerge one's own identity in that of the other, to be overwhelmed, and hence to treat oneself as less than a whole person'.[6] This seems a long way from the biblical concept of salvation which is surely to do with wholeness. It is also a long way from the biblical injunction to 'love our neighbour *as ourselves*'. How can we love ourselves if our feelings are constantly overwhelmed by the feelings of others? Low self-esteem and lack of self-acceptance do not make for healthy, wholesome relationships. 'To agree offhandedly is to place oneself in an attitude of inferiority.'[7] The reason is that always to agree with the other is to devalue one's own thoughts, feelings and ideas.

The personality can be damaged in another way, that is, by destroying the other person, by seeking for power and using the other as a footstool with which to further one's own greed. Traditionally the ruthless person is more likely to invoke criticism than the less assertive person. Indeed the latter is often commended although it is equally impossible to have a relationship with them. 'To be compliant, to abrogate one's own wishes and fit in with the desires of others even at one's own expense – how admirable, how unselfish, how "Christian"!'[8] Those brought up with this kind of piety find it difficult to understand that undue submissiveness, as well as undue assertiveness, makes a mature relationship difficult. A necessary concomitant to a lasting relationship is that it be on equal terms. Indeed, this is one of the hallmarks of maturity. In this way 'all of us come to the unity of the faith and of the knowledge of the Son of God to maturity, to the measure of the stature of Christ' (Ephesians 4.13).

On being angry

A feeling that is often suppressed in church circles is that of anger. The phrase that is used instead is 'least said soonest mended', or 'anything for a quiet life'. The speaker genuinely feels that the best thing is not to reveal the emotion but to suppress it. The implication is that if such an emotion was expressed it would be hurtful and destructive of the relationship. There is also the implicit agenda that Christians do not get angry or should not get angry, or at the very least, if they do, they should not show it. Anthony Storr writes about 'those middle class households, often professionally Christian, in which aggression is so much taboo that a cross word or a momentary loss of temper is regarded as a crime'.[9]

The taboo on expressing anger is deeply embedded within western culture, possibly arising out of the fact that it is regarded as one of the seven deadly sins. The taboo is such that many people actually deny that they ever get angry. The supposedly ideal or civilized response is always to be calm and smiling. The trouble arises

> when you have those dreadful migraines that usually come after you have visited your mother, or when your ulcer plays up, usually on the morning of the monthly conference at work, or when you are stuck in a traffic jam and you start trembling so much that you can hardly drive once the traffic starts moving.[10]

To complain about these things would be nigh impossible because you don't want to upset your family or let on to anyone at work that you do your job less than perfectly. This might invoke criticism or a withdrawal of love and affection and that can feel like a fate worse than death.

This difficulty of facing criticism can be very difficult especially for those in authority. The 'head' might well say, 'You can't please everybody all the time', but the gut feeling is 'I want to be nice to everyone.' The assumption is that if one is 'nice' to everyone then one will be totally accepted by everyone and life will be emotionally free of pain. In order to escape any kind of criticism people can avoid taking any decisions by always deferring to others. 'You do what you think is best, it doesn't put me up or down'. 'I always go along with what my wife/husband wants me to do.'

A possible way out of this dilemma is to realize that everybody enjoys complaining and so by making decisions with which other people disagree one is actually giving them scope for a great deal of enjoyment! This however is very much a 'head' solution and one is still left with the feeling of having rocked the boat and caused irreparable damage.

The ultimate difficulty for those who are fearful of offending others is reached when there is an inability to say 'no'. This can result in complete confusion. This arises because although one does not want to say no for reasons already mentioned, on the other hand a feeling of resentment can be aroused because you feel put upon or made use of, or taken for granted, and this feeling destroys any positive feeling that might have been obtained from helping someone else. A possible solution is to protect yourself against the encroachment of others. Ordained ministers have great difficulty in this area of self-protection even to the point of taking a day off each week. Ministering people are notoriously poor about keeping one day off per week sacred for themselves and their own well-being and their families. They always have a score of reasons why it cannot be done.[11] A day off becomes an optional extra rather than a necessity.

Another fear around dealing with anger is that if it is expressed it will be totally uncontrollable. Anyone who has had a series of sleepless nights with a baby knows how easy it is to harbour murderous feelings. This can be frightening. Thankfully in the majority of cases they remain as feelings, although there are many cases of baby battering. The fear is that if the anger is aroused, it will crush and damage everything and everybody that gets in its way. The false conclusion is that it is far better to suppress, subdue and control it, if not totally to deny its supposed destructive existence.

Feelings of anger and submission are closely related. A woman or man may feel unsure about being wanted and go about being submissive and pleasing in an effort to be accepted. These needy people are, in effect, begging for acceptance by offering constant placation.

> Very often such a person feels extremely frustrated and angry underneath their desire to be nice. They feel unlovable in their heart of hearts and their efforts to gain approval are geared to the knowledge that they would be dismissed if they were their true selves.[12]

This kind of person has lots of negative feelings about themselves. 'It's my fault again. Always is. Ever will be. World without end.'[13] This is the 'not OK' life position which Thomas Harris describes in his best-seller. Basically the feeling is one of inferiority; the feeling that everyone else is OK but I am most assuredly Not OK. One way of living out this life script is constantly to try to gain approval from strongly OK people. The result is that such a person becomes 'eager, willing and compliant to the demands of others'.[14] The end result is not one of lasting happiness nor a feeling of self-worth. Indeed quite the reverse tends to happen. The person's integrity has been violated and the sense of responsibility for their own life is never established. 'No matter what I do I am still Not OK.'[15]

The other side of this coin is a distorted kind of Christianity that could be stated thus. 'Thou shalt love thy neighbour better than thyself.' In the end this person becomes so hungry for love, and so frightened of appearing assertive or in any way aggressive 'that he will submerge his own personality in that of the other, and use his capacity for doing this as a kind of blackmail'.[16] Unfortunately this is a double bind situation because as Anthony Storr categorically states, 'the more a person remains dependent on others, the more aggression will be latent with in'.[17] The reason for this is that to be dependent on another person is virtually to be in the power of the other person and that power must be overcome if the person is ever to achieve the maturity of which we spoke earlier.

From a Christian point of view the disadvantage of screening off an emotion like anger is that it is then not available to us when we want it. Kenneth Slack states the case well.

There is a righteous anger which is an essential part of being human. The man who can look on cruelty and not be angry is not preserved in some sinless state of calm; he is defective in proper human emotion ... treachery, maltreatment of the weak, exploitation of the vulnerable, these and other acts ought to move us to anger. When we can look upon them with Olympian calm we have not achieved an advanced staging post on the way to sinlessness, we have begun inwardly to wither as human beings.[18]

More generally it is obviously true that we need to be able to stand up for ourselves if we are not going to be pushed around or taken advantage of. Someone who has put all their anger behind a screen will seem timid and passive and get bossed around, because their anger is not available. There are strong biological reasons for saying that anger is an emotion bred into us by countless generations of evolution in order that our survival may be ensured. Without anger our geographical territory and emotional territory would be continually encroached upon until nothing remained.[19] Paul Tournier emphasizes that aggression is not a calamity or a bad fault or a perversion but 'a force of nature present in every living thing, a gift of life which can have both beneficent and unfortunate results, depending on the use that is made of it . . . it is the very expression of life'.[20] Thus anger as a feeling cannot be said to be sinful. The results of it may be.

The part played by anger in depressive illness is well documented by Rowe[21] in families by Robin Skynner and John Cleese[22] and in the bringing up of children by John Bowlby.[23] David and Vera Mace when discussing anger in marriage say 'anger is in fact our basic survival kit, provided as a life saving resource when our very existence is threatened'.[24] The contention of the authors is that 'psychologically it is healthier to vent anger than to suppress it'.[25] It is just as natural to say 'I'm angry' as it is to say 'I'm hungry'. Alastair Campbell gives some biblical perspectives in his *Gospel of Anger*.[26]

Jesus often points out the importance of internal attitudes rather than speaking out against anger as such.

'You shall not murder, and whoever murders shall be liable to judgment. But I say to you that if you are angry with a brother or sister, you will be liable to judgment' (Matthew 5.21–22). From the perspective of God the important thing is what lies on a person's heart. Too well we know what Burns meant when he described Tam O'Shanter's wife as 'nursing her wrath to keep it warm'. This is where we nurse a grudge or quietly let it smoulder away looking for an opportunity to 'get our own back', or where resentment colours our actions, or where we think that the anger has been controlled and fool ourselves that it has been forgotten. We know too well the kind of person who puts up with everything yet forgets nothing.

The contention thus far is that our emotions are not evil or sinful. They exist. In particular we have looked at the feeling of anger and how this is often inhibited particularly in Christian circles. The Latin word *emovere* means to stir up, agitate, or move. Constantly on my retreat I was stirred up or agitated when I allowed a particular biblical text to speak to my innermost being. When my brain, as it were, was switched off, there was a different kind of revelation and insight. The right side of my brain was in operation and this is the side that often seems to function in an unconscious or involuntary way. Gerard Hughes goes so far as to suggest that if someone is not in touch with their feelings then 'making the Spiritual Exercises can be a profitless occupation, and they are unlikely to cause any lasting change in the individual'.[27]

Hughes goes on to say that feelings are intelligent. 'They are often more intelligent than our conscious minds.'[28] Moreover, 'they are the first pointers to what our hearts are most deeply desiring or most deeply fearing'.[29]

The question, which now poses itself, is whether these two seemingly different approaches can be reconciled. Is it head or heart or head and heart or some combination of the two? Strangely enough there are some clues when we consider the crucifixion of Jesus.

The cross and the clown

The third week of the Exercises can be very intense since it involves the contemplation of the sufferings of Christ. Staying with pain and suffering is not easy. Someone once said to me that he did not like going to church on Good Friday. He much preferred Easter Sunday. How right Thomas à Kempis was when he wrote,

> all desire to rejoice with Him, few are willing to endure anything for Him. Many follow Jesus unto the breaking of bread; but few to the drinking of the cup of His passion. Many revere His miracles, few follow the ignominy of His cross.[1]

More recently William Barry has written, 'Contemplation of his [Christ's] passion faces us with what we fear the most, death and its capriciousness and its often enough terrible companion, severe suffering.'[2]

The avoidance of pain is an understandable and a common phenomenon. Bereaved people often say they notice that people who hitherto had time for a chat now take avoiding action and often cross the road. They seem to be too embarrassed and do not know what to say to the bereaved. Generally speaking, women seem to be able to bear pain better than men. It was, after all, mainly women who remained at the foot of the cross. When confronted with someone who has been bereaved, or who is undergoing intense pain and suffering of whatever kind, we often find that words offer no comfort. All we can do is stay with the person and perhaps hold their hand or give them a hug. In the counselling or therapeutic relationship it is usually when the going gets tough that the patient wants to quit the process, either by not making another appointment, or within the session itself, by talking about a third party thereby fleeing from the pain of the present moment. Our brains employ all kinds of tricks and distractions in order to avoid pain. However, it is precisely at those points, if we can stay with them, that the greatest growth and change takes place. We do not usually learn very much when things are going well. It is our moments of crisis that challenge our faith and belief systems. It is precisely then that spiritual growth can take place, within the crucible of painful experiences.

Charles Elliott encourages us to enter the scene of Mary watching the crucifixion.[3] It is clear that Mary, the mother of Jesus, remains at the foot of the cross. She stays and takes in the whole horror of the scene. 'She is lacerated with all the emotion of a mother watching a favoured son, a son with the finger of God on him, die the cruellest death.'[4] How helpless and powerless she must have felt to see her son abandoned and suffering in such an abject and painful way. There is no suggestion in the Gospels that she does other than watch the terrifying spectacle of her son being subject to a horrific kind of torture. She stays with him. She does not cry out at the injustice of it all. She does not abuse the soldiers. She does not rally the support of the crowd. What must have been going through her mind?

She is aware of the hypocrisy of the crowd, some of whom were healed by Jesus. She is aware of the self-righteousness of the Pharisees and religious establishment. She is aware of the callousness of the soldiers. She is all too aware of the timidity of the disciples and of how that, above all else, hurts her son now.[5]

Entering the passion at this level is excruciating and the normal response is to run away or, at least, to resist it. If nothing else, this demonstrates how difficult prayer can be. This is not uttering a few pious phrases and then rushing on to the next round of business. It is truly meditating on the passion and beginning to open up the questions about the significance of the event for me, today.

The very idea of the cross is anathema. We want to sanitize it and underplay it and concentrate on more congenial aspects of the gospel. 'Cursed is everyone who hangs on a tree' (Galatians 3.13; cf. Deuteronomy 21.23). Yet probably *the* distinguishing mark of Christianity which sets it apart from other religions is the fact that at its heart is the worship of the crucified Christ. Christianity is sometimes described as the religion of the cross.

> Amongst the educated despisers of Christianity, this belief in a crucified Christ was merely bad taste, which was met with mockery. There is a graffito on the Palatine which represents a crucified figure with a donkey's head, and bears the inscription: 'Alexamenos worships his God'.[6]

In other words the symbol of the cross was not a sign of victory. Far from it. It was a symbol of derision: 'a stumbling block to Jews and foolishness to the Gentiles' (1 Corinthians 1.23). Moreover, 'the symbol of the cross in the church points to the God who was crucified not between two candles on an altar, but between two thieves in the place of the skull, where the outcasts belong, outside the gates of the city'.[7]

However as Alan Jones says, 'to know God is to suffer God'[8] and he then goes on to quote Jürgen Moltmann:

> to suffer God means experiencing in oneself the death pangs of the old ... and the birth pangs of the new ...
> The closer people come to the divine reality, the more

deeply they are drawn into this dying and rebirth . . .
Christian meditation and contemplation are therefore at
their very heart *meditatio crucis*, meditation on the
passion.[9]

The corollary to this entering of the passion is that we can
then more deeply enter into the experience of the Living
Christ.

Clowns for God and the folly of the cross

At the end of this phase of the Exercises I felt utterly
drained. There had been times when I just did not want to
carry on with the meditations. To be constantly aware of
so much pain and hurt and suffering was almost intoler-
able. My mind often employed distractions to deaden the
hurt. I remember vividly on a number of occasions actually
thinking about clowns in the midst of all the heartache. At
first blush this may not seem a very Ignatian thing to do,
but on the other hand a strong emphasis of Ignatian
spirituality is that God is in all things. If I was thinking and
dreaming about clowns then God was surely in the
experience somewhere. Certainly, during my ministry, I
had preached a number of times on the foolishness of the
cross. That act of preaching, though, was a very cerebral
process. However, on another occasion, I had been put in
touch with the clown within myself not by thinking about
it but by actually feeling what it was like to be a clown.
That needs some explanation.

My first introduction to clowning came when I attended
a conference for chaplains in higher education. The
underlying theme of the conference was 'circus skills and
the work of a chaplain'. There were workshops on juggling
(the need to keep several balls in the air at the same time
due to the demands of home life, family life, prayer life,
pastoral visits, service preparation and so on), and on tight
rope walking (the Christian life sometimes feels like

balancing on a very high tight rope: Will I slip and fall to the depths below or will I be supported by a safety net?). To my surprise I found myself in a workshop for those aspiring to be clowns.

I thoroughly enjoyed these workshops until the leader, a professional clown, began to show us how to put make-up on, and then invited us to do so. This I resisted. Of course I had preached on the text about being a 'fool for Christ's sake', and I knew with my head the importance of the image but actually trying to be a clown felt unnecessary and quite ludicrous. I strongly resisted any suggestion of being a clown. I wanted to be in control. A good cerebral discussion felt far safer. However, in the course of time, common sense lost ground and I started to become a clown.

One does not, as it were, put on any old face. Part of the secret is to discover the clown which we all have within us.[10] This takes time. One has to respond to the deep feelings within. In the course of the next few weeks I discovered that my alter ego was Zeno, a tramp clown. My first experience as a clown at the conference was when a group of us visited the local hostelry. What an experience. Most people ignored us, some were plainly embarrassed and only one person was brave enough to speak to us. It reminded me very much of the reactions one can provoke when going into a crowded place with a dog collar on. I was beginning to gain a different perspective on my work as a minister.

Many months later I was to enter a church service halfway through dressed as Zeno. Never have I felt so vulnerable. Where could I sit? What book should I use? My clothes did not seem appropriate. What would people say? Would they be friendly and receptive? Would they laugh or turn a cold shoulder? What on earth am I doing here? Is this how people feel when they go into church for the very first time? It is enormously difficult to cross the threshold of a church. Why should this be when we claim to be a company of sinners loving everybody, not a fellowship of saints loving each other? There is no doubt that being a clown puts one in touch with a great feeling of vulnerability. 'It is that aloneness, that sinking sense of being unloved, and, worse, unlovable, that lies at the heart of the clown's vulnerability.'[11]

> The clown is the vulnerable lover, constantly risking everything for his love; danger, ridicule, even death. He will joke, poke fun, ridicule but always with himself as the object, the target, never the audience. It is for us to risk making the connection between the clown and ourselves. We can begin to meet the clown, the child within.[12]

Of course the main contribution of the clown is that he makes people laugh. Someone has described laughter as 'internal jogging'. Laughter is very powerful. It releases the emotions and reduces stress. The clown is a great laughter-maker. But it is not laughing at people, it is not cruel or sick humour. Somehow the clown gets people to laugh at themselves. When the great circus acts come on we say, 'How can they do it?', but when the clowns come on we say, 'They are like us.' We know what it is like to be laughed at, to have tripped up, to feel awkward, to have dropped something and, metaphorically, to have had our trousers fall down or to have a custard pie thrown at us and have had 'egg on our face'. Somehow the clown gets people to laugh at themselves. This could be the beginning of forgiveness. Harvey Cox in a chapter on Christ the Harlequin describes laughter as 'the voice of faith'.[13] This is where laughter is real and not 'strained, cruel, artificial or merely habitual'. This is the kind of laughter that does not hide our true feelings.

It can be seen then that becoming a clown puts one in touch with feelings and puts the audience in touch with theirs. This theme was precisely the hidden agenda in my retreat. For this to happen it is necessary once again to become childlike. Not 'childish, throwing tantrums every hour on the hour, though it needs to be said we've got to come to terms with anger and rage and not just bury it to appear later as ulcers or breakdowns',[14] but childlike in the sense of being open, vulnerable, questioning and trusting. A.V. Campbell in a chapter on 'Wise Folly' writes:

> Jesus surely appears to be the greatest of fools when he asks God to forgive his accusers and executioners even as they mock him in his suffering. How could a person allow himself to be so exploited, unless he trusted beyond reason, in the ultimate triumph of love?[15]

Here again, coming from a different angle is the trusting 'beyond reason'. This is the spontaneity which is not only a hallmark of a clown it is also a hallmark of prayer.

'Prayer isn't a top-level board meeting between two frightfully important people, it is a form of play in which friendship is formed and trust is forged, and it must be entered upon playfully lest it be reduced to the muttered mumbo-jumbo that the world presumes it to be already.'[16] In prayer different rules apply and we can all too readily fall into the trap of saying our prayers with a host of words rather than praying. To pray with the head alone leaves out that most important part of our humanity, our heart, without which we would all wither and die. 'It is with our heart of hearts that we see the heart of the world.'[17]

The conference where my clown experience began concluded with a magnificent 'circus' celebration of the Lord's Supper. Participants were dressed in clothes appropriate to their particular workshop and so I, naturally, was dressed as a clown. To begin with there were very few words and lots of dance and movement in typical circus fashion. There was a feeling of joy and freedom. However the atmosphere of the worship changed when we came to the actual remembrance of the Last Supper.

Through my clown eyes I could feel this very clearly. What was a service of joy and celebration and spoke to the heart became a stodgy diet of words. Celebration became cerebration. We had jumped into the head. The words of the great eucharistic prayer of thanksgiving became a long, protracted dirge, which felt entirely inappropriate in that setting.

> When outdated words in our liturgies and doctrines strike us as funny, then we need to laugh at our own faulty attempts to figure God out. And when we find ourselves getting angry when someone presents something funny during worship, then we need to laugh at ourselves for taking ourselves too seriously. Worship involves bringing our entire selves before God. Our solemn sides are not more holy or acceptable to God than our bumbling, error-prone ways. I have to remind myself of this often because I think there is so much at stake. Well, there is a lot at stake, it's our humanity and faith.[18]

The bread and wine were taken round by the officiants. I was overcome by the feeling of uncertainty over whether it was acceptable for me to receive the bread. After all, as a clown, I felt very much on the edge of what was going on. Clowns tend not to be a major act. They are sideshows, relieving the tension between the elephants, the lions and the flying trapeze. 'Clowns are not in the centre of the events. They appear between the great acts, fumble and fall, and make us smile again after the tensions created by the heroes we came to admire.'[19] What more marginalized place can there be than being crucified between two thieves outside the city wall in the place of a skull? Clowns have no authority, yet the church very often hangs on to authority and the structures of hierarchy. The Son of Man had nowhere to lay his head. Jesus did not live in a palace or dress in ecclesiastical finery.

As the service progressed I became very uncomfortable at another point. It seemed very strange to me, as a clown, that the officiants completed the Eucharist by eating and drinking what was left of the bread and wine. I agree that my nonconformist prejudices and predilections came into play at this point, but it did not seem to fit with the prevailing ambience. Circuses are places where people share and look after one another, there is an interdependence. It did not seem right that some people, in authority, were having more than the rest. In any case, I was hungry. Those on the margins often are.

The final act of worship, which seemed to add insult to my very injured clown, was when we sang the last hymn like a funeral dirge. The only response, which my clown could make, was to take my hat off and pretend to take the offertory. The clown within me enabled me to diffuse the situation and lighten up a service, which had become very heavy. When people come into church they very often leave their humanity behind on the church steps. We somehow feel that entirely human responses like laughing and clapping are inappropriate. Yet, worship above all else is an offering of our whole selves to God, our hearts as well as our heads. To this extent worship is an enormous act of celebration.

Look carefully at the next great ecclesiastical event in your area. What is its message? Does it speak of hope, heaven, of colour and riches beyond compare, or does it weep with a kind of weariness, of hanging on to the past, of status and privilege?[20]

The same writer, Patrick Forbes, describes the church as a 'hot-air balloon, powered into the sky by the heat of a thousand inappropriate sermons'.[21]

The church and its members have often been the butt of satire. In the sixteenth century Erasmus wrote his classic book *Praise of Folly* in which he says that the world has to be saved by foolishness. He describes theologians as a 'remarkably supercilious and touchy lot'[22] and more pertinently for our purposes that 'all who look for a bit of gaiety and fun in life keep their doors firmly shut against the wise'.[23] For Erasmus the image of Christ as a fool is central:

> Christ, too, though he is the wisdom of the Father, was made something of a fool himself in order to help the folly of mankind, when he assumed the nature of man and was seen in man's form; just as he was made sin so that he could redeem sinners. Nor did he wish them to be redeemed in any other way save by the folly of the cross and through his simple, ignorant apostles, to whom he unfailingly preached folly.[24]

Jesus preached that the last would be first, that we should love our enemies, turn the other cheek and go the extra mile, that you have to lose your life in order to save it. He upset the moneychangers in the temple, walked across water and entered Jerusalem upon a donkey.

> Who but a clown would want to move mountains or calm the raging seas? Who but a clown could envisage camels wriggling through eyes of needles and wolves prancing about in sheep's clothing? Who but a clown could get away with all he said about the scribes and Pharisees?[25]

The Christian life is full of ups and downs, hurts, temptations, pain and suffering but there is also the promise of victory. God refuses to let Christ remain dead and raises him to a new life, and 'Christ not staying dead was a very clownish thing to do.'[26]

A mystery

Whatever we make of the cross it stands there as a matter of historical fact, as a challenge. In talking about evidence for the existence of God it is something we have to come to terms with, yet our minds struggle to comprehend it. 'Reason, philosophies and theologies of the problem of evil can only nibble at its surface. The mystery of Christ's passion and death upsets all our theories.'[27] Yet the power of the cross is succinctly put by Paul: 'for God's foolishness is wiser than human wisdom, and God's weakness is stronger than human strength' (1 Corinthians 1.25). God in Christ refuses to exert power and takes the form of a slave thereby identifying himself with all human beings. He 'emptied himself, taking the form of a slave, being born in human likeness. And being found in human form, he humbled himself and became obedient to the point of death, even death on a cross' (Philippians 2.7–8).

The power of the cross lies in the mystery of God's gracious act of love and self-sacrifice. 'God so loved the world that he gave his only Son' (John 3.16). The writer of the Fourth Gospel goes on to say that God sent his Son into the world 'not to condemn the world, but that the world might be saved through him'. In other words 'for a believer to urge the exclusive claims of Christ in a bullying offensive, and triumphalist manner is to deny the very Spirit of the Christ one is proclaiming. Christ bullies no one. The cross coerces no one.'[28]

The cost

This love came home to me with great force when during the retreat I thought about the cost. I had taken the decision to deprive myself of all the things I hold dear, especially my wife, family and the comforts of home life. There was also a not inconsiderable financial cost. Of course, I knew that self-denial and sacrifice are basic ingredients in the Christian life, but I had to learn the hard way that love in its profoundest sense means letting go. 'Learning to love is learning to renounce the other for the sake of the other.'[29] In other words love is not possession. Kahlil Gibran says in a passage on marriage 'love one another, but make not a bond of love'.[30] In speaking of children he says:

> your children are not your children. They are the sons and daughters of Life's longing for itself. They come through you but not from you. And though they are with you yet they belong not to you . . . you are the bows from which your children as living arrows are sent forth.[31]

Love is learning to live:

> without possession, manipulation, and control. I can possess an autumn day or a beautiful view of fruit trees in blossom no more that I can possess my wife or my children. Learning to love without possession and finding that one is loved without conditions is what it is to receive the gift of tears and to be surprised by joy.[32]

There are, then, no conditions surrounding love. God's love is just the same. He loves us as we are. The cost of this can sometimes be overwhelming but when I contemplated the 'cost' of my retreat it was nothing compared to the cost of God's self-sacrificial gift of himself. Of course this kind of love 'leaves us open to wounding and disappointment. It makes us ready to suffer. It leads us out of isolation into a fellowship with others, with people different from ourselves, and this fellowship is always associated with suffering.'[33]

In conclusion, if we are really to enter into the passion of Christ we can only do so when we have let go of everything to which we cling. Maybe we try to cling with our heads and try to understand the mystery of the cross. Ultimately this avenue proves to be a cul-de-sac. When we enter the passion at the level of our feelings, then we can be touched in the depth of our souls. We can experience the gift of tears as I did on many occasions. This is all part of the cost but it is a price worth paying.

All Christians are called to believe in the foolishness of the cross and this makes clowns of us all.

A Fool's Prayer

Father, God of Fools,
   Lord of Clowns and Smiling Saints,
   I rejoice in this playful prayer
   that you are a God of laugher and of tears.
Blessed are You, for You have rooted within me
   the gifts of humour, lightheartedness and mirth.
With jokes and comedy, You cause my heart to sing
   as laughter is made to flow out of me.

I am grateful that Your Son, Jesus,
   who was this world's master of wit,
   daily invites me to be a fool for Your sake,
   to embrace the madness
   of Your prophets, holy people and saints.

I delight in that holy madness
   which becomes the very medicine
   to heal the chaos of the cosmos
   since it calls each of us
   out of the humdrumness of daily life
   into joy, adventure,
   and, most of all, into freedom.

I, who am so easily tempted to barter my freedom
   for tiny speckles of honour and power,
   am filled with gratitude that Your Son's very life
   has reminded me to value only love,

and communion with other persons and with You,
and to balance honour with humour.

With circus bands and organ grinders,
    with fools, clowns, court-jesters, and comics,
    with high-spirited angels and saints,
    I too join the fun and foolishness of life,
    so that Your holy laughter
    may ring out to the edges of the universe.

Blessed are You, Lord my God,
    who invited me to be a holy fool.
Amen.[34]

Head or heart?

The little prince went away to look at the roses again.

'You are not at all like my rose,' he said. 'As yet you are nothing. No one has tamed you, and you have tamed no one. You are like my fox when I first knew him. He was only a fox like a hundred thousand other foxes. But I have made him my friend, and now he is unique in all the world.'

And the roses were very much embarrassed.

'You are beautiful, but you are empty,' he went on. 'One could not die for you. To be sure an ordinary passer-by would think that my rose looked just like you – the rose that belongs to me. But in herself alone she is more important than all the hundreds of you other roses: because it is she that I have watered; because it is she that I have put under the glass globe; because it is she that I have sheltered behind the screen; because it is for her that I have killed the caterpillars (except the two or three that we saved to become butterflies); because it is she that I have listened to, when she grumbled, or boasted, or even sometimes when she said nothing. Because she is *my* rose.'

And he went back to meet the fox.

'Good-bye,' he said.

'Good-bye,' said the fox. 'And now here is my secret, a very simple secret: It is only with the heart that one can see rightly; what is essential is invisible to the eye.'[1]

Germans have a saying: *Die Rose ist ohne warum. Sie*

bluhet weil sie bluhet. 'The rose has no whys; it blossoms because it blossoms.'

This leaves me with the problem of where do we put our questions – the whys, whens, and whats of biblical criticism and historical analysis? I want to know with my head whether the Bible is true. What really happened all those many years ago in far-off Palestine? I have been brought up and educated to ask questions and to not be afraid of questions because this is a part of my search for the Truth and God is where the Truth is found. Surely God reveals himself in our questioning and probing?

Of course, for some people the very act of questioning is a betrayal of faith. When the books *Honest to God* and *The Myth of God Incarnate* were published they created a great furore among the faithful. Statements from the former Bishop of Durham, David Jenkins, often cause great disturbance even though he is only saying what biblical scholars have been writing about for years. I am certainly unhappy when people take the Bible at face value. We live in a completely different world from that which Jesus inhabited. For example, Jesus expected the end of the world very soon, yet we take out insurance policies. This is an obvious denial of the fact that we expect the world to end in the near future. Jesus believed in demonic possession. We utilize medicines for epilepsy. How we perceive certain kinds of behaviour is affected by our different understandings, which have different practical outcomes. If someone fell down with an attack of epilepsy in the Middle East in the time of Jesus, this behaviour would naturally have been understood as due to possession by an evil spirit and he or she would probably have been exorcised. The same behaviour pattern today would be understood in terms of an unco-ordinated discharge of motor neurones and the person treated with a medicinal drug.

My problem then is that I do not, as it were, want to commit intellectual suicide nor do I want to be charged with anti-intellectualism. There is evidence from a few years ago to suggest that theological college students neither attain, nor aspire to, academic competence.[2] Moreover there is a kind of student with a 'shut mind' who is not open to development and growth.[3] Training seems to have little effect on such people. Books are shut at the end of a course never to be reopened. Yet the Christian faith is always throwing up questions especially those to do with the problems of suffering and evil and how God works in the world. To deny my intellect the opportunity to work at some of these questions would be to deny an important part of myself. Is Christianity simply a 'leap of the heart' and for this to happen do I need to cut off my head? Is reason a whore, as Luther is reported to have said?

There is certainly a distinguished number who allege that Christianity is first and foremost a religion of the heart. Petru Dumitriu talks about the 'certitude of the heart'.[4] Thomas Merton says that in the 'prayer of the heart' we do not 'reason about dogmas of faith ... we seek rather to gain a direct existential grasp, a personal experience of the deepest truths of life and faith'. Purity of heart is an 'unconditional and totally humble surrender to God, a total acceptance of ourselves and of our situation as willed by him'.[5] Blaise Pascal was a great mathematician and scientific thinker. He admitted that 'the last step of reason is to recognise that there are many things which lie beyond it'. The great medieval theologian Thomas Aquinas said that all his books on theology were 'so much straw' in comparison to what he knew of God in prayer. Certainly in monastic prayer and the tradition of the Desert Fathers the heart plays a central role in prayer.

In that classic book of Christian mysticism *The Cloud of Unknowing*, we are told that God 'may well be loved, but not thought. By love he can be caught and held, but by thinking never'.[6] Julian of Norwich writes, 'it is the will of the Lord that our prayer and our trust be large. We must truly know that our Lord is the ground from which our prayer sprouts and that it is a gift given out of love, otherwise we waste our time and pain ourselves.'[7] John of the Cross says that 'faith is the first garment to be put on'.[8]

In this century Simone Weil has written that 'the special function of the intelligence requires total liberty, implying the right to deny everything, and allowing of no domination. Wherever it usurps control there is an excess of individualism.'[9] Hans Urs von Balthasar says that 'the person contemplating will use the faculties of the "inner senses" and imagination to call up the image of the Incarnate Word – Jesus.'[10] Petru Dumitriu says that 'all description of prayer, with full awareness of what one is talking about, is paradoxical and so it has no logical sense. All logical analysis of prayer is absurdity and foolishness before personal experience of prayer; it is like a blind man pronouncing on the colour in a Van Gogh.'[11]

These are powerful indications implying that the heart has the ascendancy over the intellect. It is to assent to the notion that prayer is 'heart speaking to heart'. This is not a surprising conclusion. Intellectual inquiry does not lead a person to a knowledge of God. Listening to a sermon does not usually bring about an inner change. In the main congregations live their lives as they did before. Inner change begins to happen when we appropriate an idea or experience at a deeper level of our being than in our heads. It is like giving people advice. The advice can be accepted with the head, but if it is not taken on board at a much deeper level the advice will not be followed. Change happens when an idea is 'taken on board', when the idea, or concept, is internalized into the heart. A question can be discussed endlessly but it will not in itself effect change until there is a change in the heart. For example, the question of world poverty has been discussed endlessly and we have the resources to eradicate poverty, but nothing happens because there is no real desire for change to happen. After all the rich may find themselves getting poorer. In the meantime the rich get richer and the poor are getting poorer.

However I am still left with a feeling of dissatisfaction. Even if one allows for the predominance of the heart I am still unsure where that leaves the intellect. I know with Paul that 'we know only in part' (1 Corinthians 13.9). I know also that people are far more moved by the example, say, of Mother Teresa, or Martin Luther King or, indeed, simple acts of neighbourly kindness, than by tomes of systematic theology, but I am still left with the question of the place of the intellect.

Poets, musicians and artists would argue that in their works they are trying to reach the deeper levels of the human psyche and although rational analysis is useful, in the end it is the 'tingle' factor that matters. On one occasion T.S. Eliot was asked at a party what he meant by his line 'lady, three white leopards sat under a juniper tree'. After a pregnant pause he replied, 'I meant, "lady, three white leopards sat under a juniper tree".'[12] The poet had said precisely what he wanted to say and there is no way in which he could improve upon it. When we listen to a Beethoven symphony what does it mean? Do we hear what the composer intended and does it matter so long as our emotions are stirred? We can read the programme notes but they may not mean very much. They may not add to our enjoyment of the music and could actually detract from it. We certainly do not ask questions such as 'When did it happen?' and 'Did it actually happen?' Music and poetry are there to be enjoyed. If they do not affect us we move on to something that does.

In a similar fashion Rubem Alves asks the question about a Gothic cathedral. 'What is its meaning? What did the architect have in mind?'[13] We can pursue all kinds of investigations to discover the answer to these questions but in the final analysis knowledge fails to lift us to appreciate the 'vast, empty spaces, its silence, the light which fractures through iridescent glasses, the darkness which plays with the dance of the candles and gives movement to the stones'.[14]

To be more specific we have to determine the place of biblical scholarship. I remain unhappy about a text meaning just what it says to me in the here and now. We can be deceived by our own reasoning powers, but we can also be misled by our feelings. Simply being open to a text can mean that we interpret it in the light of our own prejudices. In this way the evil regime of apartheid in South Africa was supported by a biblical misunderstanding. Furthermore such an approach leaves one prey to the charge of subjectivism and individualism. This is far removed from the primacy of the group or congregation, body or vine, in the Bible.

Biblical criticism attempts to determine the meaning that a text had: What the text originally meant. The scholar tries to answer the questions, 'What did the author originally intend?', 'Who was the author?', 'Who was he addressing?', 'What was the context?', and so on. Scholarship tries to determine the meanings of the original symbols that in many cases appear quite foreign to the twentieth-century mind. All this is valuable work and provides insights that would otherwise be lost. Sometimes scholars disagree and the text is open to different interpretations. In the last analysis the important thing is not, What did it mean then?, but what does it mean now? If we treat the text solely as 'out there' it becomes like a murder mystery to be solved. As soon as we know 'who has done it' the story loses its power and it would be meaningless to read it again. There is nothing more to be said. Leaving things open is an opportunity for the reader to appropriate the text for himself or herself. This is the difference between talking about something and actually knowing something inside. There is a difference between what we are taught and what our heart tells us is true.

I can only say that during my retreat I often had the profound experience of being encountered by God. This kind of encounter is what Martin Buber has called the 'I–Thou' relationship.[15] It happens when we experience 'the other' beyond our perceptions. This 'other' does not depend for its existence on our mental framework. Indeed we have to let go of our ideas and conceptual structure for the encounter to take place, only in that way can we be open to the unexpected. Indeed we have to 'unlearn in order to learn anew'.[16] We cannot stage manage or control this encounter. The hymn says 'only believe and thou shalt see',[17] but we cannot force ourselves to believe. Just as, at the end of the day, we cannot survive on the faith of our parents. God has no stepchildren, only children.

While meditating on the Exercises it struck me that these experiences of being 'touched' could not have been contrived by logical analysis or deduction. Quite the reverse. I was often left speechless and could only wonder. This is the unknown God, the God of mystery, who cannot be apprehended by logical thought. Yet the work of the heart involves questioning. We need to check whether an experience really is of God or whether it is necessary to postulate God at all. Was I fooling myself? Was it really God speaking or was I speaking to myself? Was God a convenient description to explain things that defied rational description? Could this experience have been a projection of my innermost desires and feelings? The teaching of Ignatius includes that of learning to discern the movements of the spirit. One test is whether the experience is creative or destructive. God loves us and desires only the best for us and therefore if the experience is destructive and producing great agitation, it is not of God. God wants to create, not destroy. He wants to make us whole personalities, not provide routes by which we escape from the realities of everyday living.

I have to fall back on to the authority of my experiences which, it should be said, were in no way a product of group pressures. My experiences took place in complete solitude. As a one-time psychologist I do not find this easy. Nor is the experience subject to the usual rigours of experimental proof. In my defence I can say that more than 36 per cent of a national poll sample said that at some time they had been aware of or influenced by a presence or a power.[18] On that basis we could say that about a third of the population aged over 16 have had a similar kind of experience. One of the earliest psychologists wrote a fascinating book about religious experience. Towards the end he wrote 'there is actually and literally more life in our total soul that we are at any time aware of',[19] and the essential part of religion is 'the fact that the conscious person is continuous with a wider self through which saving experiences come'.[20]

The final kind of evidence for the experience comes from what Petru Dumitriu calls the:

> evidence of grace. It cannot be seen, it cannot be verified, it cannot be induced, it does not come whenever we choose to experiment with it, but it is there – grace, the instant of gratitude in which the great unknown context itself is found again in my consciousness and in my heart, with perfect intellectual clarity, in perfect emotional transparency. Am I going to deny it . . . ?[21]

Here is the experience of the head and the heart coming together. The head recognizes that God is a given and the heart opens itself to his presence. The synthesis then is the 'head in the heart' or the 'heart in the head'. 'Prayer is to stand before God with the head in the heart';[22] or as Anthony de Mello puts it 'lose your mind and come to your senses'.[23] Seeing is not believing. Only believing is believing. This is a gift from God.

A possible route into this kind of experience is to become childlike. Unfortunately the church has a habit of keeping people in a state of childishness. Congregations often defer to the minister and do not accept their own responsibilities. For example, it is assumed that the minister will know when someone is ill. The person feels somewhat 'miffed' when he or she does not pay them a pastoral visit. The minister was unaware of the situation and they had not taken the responsibility to tell him or her. There is often in the church an unhealthy fear of authority. However becoming childlike is not the same as being infantile. 'It takes a spiritually mature person to enter the Kingdom of God as a little child.'[24] This is the experience of being reborn and being touched by the power of the wind of the Spirit.

> No here nor now can touch
> God, who is nothingness,
> The more we reach for him,
> The more he vanishes.
>
> See, where thou nothing seest;
> Go, where thou canst not go;
> Hear, where there is no sound;
> Then where God speaks art thou.[25]

This question of when God speaks brings us to the whole issue of discernment.

8

Discerning God's will

The phrase 'thy will be done' slips easily off the tongue as the words of the Lord's Prayer are rushed through. We pray that God's will is done as we offer our prayers to him and we seek to order our business meetings so that all is done according to his will. It is perhaps obvious that a mature Christian would want to do the will of God, but does God have a will? Certainly Jesus thought so. He says in the Fourth Gospel 'My food is to do the will of him who sent me and to complete his work'(John 4.34). 'I can do nothing on my own. As I hear, I judge; and my judgment is just, because I seek to do not my own will but the will of him who sent me'(John 5.30). There is also the example in the account of Jesus in the garden of Gethsemane. 'Father, for you all things are possible; remove this cup from me; yet not what I want, but what you want'(Mark 14.36). These references give a clear indication that Jesus thought that God had a will and insofar as the task of a mature Christian is to follow and imitate the life of Christ it follows that we also have to do the will of God.

The problem is that it becomes quite easy to suggest that God's will is fixed and final rather like the script of a play. All Christians have to do is to learn the lines, so to speak, and everything will be all right. 'Sometimes people talk about the will of God as if it were a large, immensely complex, ever-changing, living blue-print of what God 'wants' to happen in the world.'[1] This can produce great difficulty for the ardent believer who tries to discover the lines and learn them and then suffers pangs of guilt or remorse if it is once thought that the lines are not the correct ones. Furthermore this scenario implies that God's will is intransigent: That he only has one will. If that is the case where does that leave human freedom, and where also does that leave the human ability to discern? We shall look at each of these problems in turn.

From a psychological point of view, ever since the time of Freud, it is all too apparent that many of our actions are determined by our early childhood experiences. All of us are subject to forces impinging on us from our un-conscious. Behaviourist psychologists would deny the importance of the unconscious, even its existence, and would assert that human beings are conditioned by their environment, and their potential is limited by their genetic make-up. To that extent, no one is a free agent. At the other end of the spectrum an existential psychologist would assert that humans have total free choice and responsibility.

The Christian position has always been to assert a degree of freedom within humans but at the same time recognizing that this freedom is limited. 'No one was more aware of this than Augustine, who stressed the pressure which 'the flesh' exercised on human freedom.'[2] Clearly there are certain indisputable determinants of behaviour, for example, the structure of our brains and central nervous system, our early childhood experiences, our genetic struc-ture and so on; nevertheless within these limits we all exhibit a degree of personal responsibility, moral choice and freedom. In other words we have the possibility of discernment. We shall discover that the process of discernment as understood in the Ignatian sense, in fact, leads to a greater degree of freedom.

The process of discernment

In the process of discernment the object is to discover God's will but it is not to discover that will for the whole of one's life but simply for a given situation. Discernment in this sense is about discovering what God wants you to do in a particular concrete situation. Furthermore it is about what is necessary for that person to do rather than what God aims to do to that person. 'In his way of finding God's will, Ignatius is not proposing a way of finding any universal moral principle or rules applicable to all persons or to some class or persons or to some class of situations or cases.'[3] Discernment, then, is for a particular individual in a particular situation, given their individual gifts, personality, temperament, character and circumstances. Furthermore, it is only the individual who can make that discernment. It cannot be done, as it were, by a third party.

The process of discernment is carried out within a setting which presupposes God's love – 'a willingness to look at and appreciate the signs of God's love for us and in response to listen to the voice of the Spirit of God and to follow where the Spirit leads'.[4] It is assumed that the 'voice of God' is calling for a free, personal response. The person is free to do or not to do what God prefers. 'It is a call not merely to do some act but to choose freely that act rather than some other real alternative and to choose it because it is what God prefers.'[5] Any choice, of course, in this context is between two morally acceptable courses of action (#170).[6]

Ignatius also says that certain things fall into the category of an unchangeable choice, such as marriage, and the priesthood (# 171). It goes without saying that he was writing from within the culture of the sixteenth century. Many people would argue today that even such things as marriage and the priesthood could only be chosen at a particular time. In the course of time these decisions have to be 'checked-out' to see if the original choice is still valid. Vocations and relationships are not static. They need to be continually chosen existentially as ongoing realities. As stated above, discernment is only for a particular time, it is not prophetic. Circumstances may change.

For Ignatius the intention of any choice is simple. 'I must

consider only the end for which I am created, that is, for the praise of God our Lord and for the salvation of my soul. Hence, whatever I choose must help me to this end for which I am created' (#169). In a very real sense it is important to be aware of one's identity before a choice can be made. Indeed identity must precede choice. All too often it is the other way round in our society – we make choices and these choices then determine the kind of person we are. However, in Ignatian discernment a choice is made knowing that one is a child of God. There is a desire to draw close to God and to act as a mature Christian.

Another way of putting this is that the process involves looking for the insights and movements that lead to a more authentic lifestyle. Where is your deepest self engaged? What is it that brings you to life? Where is the fount of your energy? It was the genius of Ignatius to discover the link between making a choice and discerning the movement of spirits within. This he discovered, as we saw in Chapter 1, when he was convalescing after being severely wounded by a cannonball while serving as a soldier. Ignatius used the terminology of good and bad spirits. It has been argued that it was this discernment of different spirits, which began his conversion. Indeed Barry and Connolly assert that 'at its most basic level discernment consists of recognizing differences'.[7]

Today it is more appropriate to talk about different feelings. It is a fundamental conviction underlying Ignatian discernment that God communicates himself to people through feelings and ideas, but especially through feelings. As we have seen earlier the problem here is that we live in a culture which underestimates feelings. However the first step is to acknowledge that we have feelings. We may not be able to name them, let alone express them, but we all have them. Moreover as Barry says 'there is an inner logic in our affections that leads to the heart of reality and that can be discovered through a disciplined attention to our experience'.[8]

The process of discernment which Ignatius describes occurs in the Exercises. These Exercises, as we have noted, begin with the 'First Principle and Foundation' which states 'human beings are created to praise, reverence and serve God our Lord . . . to do this, I must make myself indifferent to all created things, in regard to everything which is left to my freedom of will . . . I ought to desire and elect only the thing which is more conducive to the end for which I am created' (## 23).

It can be seen that Ignatius clearly assumes that some freedom is a given in the Christian life and that choices can therefore be made. Indeed it could be argued that the Exercises are intended to bring us into a position of freedom with respect to ourselves, other people and God. For example, English says:

> the Exercises are an instrument to help a person to come to freedom. The kind of freedom I am speaking about is a kind of realized, existential freedom – freedom with oneself, and freedom within oneself. It might be called 'ultimate freedom', the freedom that accompanies deep awareness of the ultimate meaning of one's life.[9]

This kind of freedom in the Christian sense implies 'an acceptance of oneself as historically coming from God, going to God and being with God'.[10] It is probably true to say such existential freedom can only be experienced within the love of God. Words like peace, self-awareness, identity and 'shalom' spring to mind. As can be seen from the First Principle and Foundation quoted above, Ignatius uses the important word 'indifference'.

This word in our society holds negative connotations and carries with it a meaning like apathy. In the Ignatian sense it does not mean this. Nor does it mean being indifferent to people or that we should be unfeeling and unresponsive people. A more apt meaning for us would be openness to all possibilities, so that God can draw us to where he wants us to be. We can only be where God wants us to be if we are truly indifferent. To this extent there is a need to be flexible. Ignatius says that we must be indifferent even to those things that are close to our biological and psychological make-up. 'Consequently, we should not prefer health to sickness, riches to poverty, honour to dishonour, a long life to a short life. The same holds for all other things' (# 23). As we have seen the attainment of this indifference or spiritual freedom may make itself felt at the end of the Exercises but in any event there needs to be much prayer and the gift of the grace of God.

Of course this idea runs counter to the values of the world. Any 'normal' person would prefer the reverse of these values, that is, health to sickness, riches to poverty and so on. Indeed we are urged to lead healthy lives and to attain wealth in one way or another and then we will indeed be truly happy. The problem is that these attainments become gods, addictions or obsessions and we lose our inner freedom. Furthermore there is a tension between the values of this world and the perspective of God. He loves all equally. He is impartial to whether people are healthy, educated, young or old. God has no favourites. He is indifferent.

The Ignatian concept of indifference is remarkably like the sentiments found in the Methodist covenant service.

Put me to what you will, rank me with whom you will; put me to doing, put me to suffering; let me be employed for you or laid aside for you, exalted for you or brought low for you; let me be full, let me be empty; let me have all things, let me have nothing; I freely and wholeheartedly yield all things to your pleasure and disposal. And now, glorious and blessed God, Father, Son, and Holy Spirit, you are mine and I am yours.[11]

Of course, Paul had similar sentiments when he wrote to

the Philippians 'not that I am referring to being in need; for I have learned to be content with whatever I have I know what it is to have plenty. In any and all circumstances I have learned the secret of being well-fed and of going hungry, of having plenty and of being in need. I can do all things through him who strengthens me' (Philippians 4.11–13).

Ignatius' own description of indifference is 'as a balance at equilibrium, without leaning to one side or the other' (#15). In other words it is about cultivating a sense of poise so that we are ready to go in the direction that God indicates. It is this indifference which is crucial in any consideration of freedom or the desire to do the will of God. The other crucial attitude in Ignatian discernment is to do with humility. Indeed before entering upon what is called 'the election' or the 'choice of a state in life', there is an exercise which amounts to a consideration of three kinds of humility (#165–68). It could equally well be called the three degrees of indifference or the three degrees of freedom. The object of this exercise is to free the person from fears, deceptions and misguided generosity. 'In all spiritual matters, the more one divests oneself of self-love, self-will, and self-interests, the more progress one will make' (##189). Of course, we can only desire this kind of freedom. We cannot attain it but we can receive it as pure gift.

It is important to note that indifference is not to do with being passive, or apathetic and certainly it is not about being indifferent to evil. Indifference is not lovelessness nor is it a lack of sympathy. Indifference 'is essentially an alacrity, openness and alertness of spirit to a God who is lovingly committed to history'.[12] It is an inner openness to serve God whatever the cost. 'Ignatian indifference is always a means, never an end in itself. Which must change into non-indifference once God manifests the means for his better service and praise.'[13]

It is difficult to attain this level of indifference simply

because of our 'attachments'. In discerning a way forward we often present God with a list of conditions. 'I will be happy to work wherever you want me to Lord just as long as I am near my ageing family, my children are near a good school, the house is in a good neighbourhood and it is not too far away from Manchester because I support Manchester United.' This may be overstating the case but the general picture is true. Anthony de Mello writes that 'an attachment is a belief that without something you are not going to be happy'.[14] It is very similar to desire or craving and while these feelings prevail there is no possibility of attaining indifference. It is very difficult for discernment to take place. As de Mello writes 'attachments are blind. Clinging, craving, and desire are blind'.[15] He defines love as 'the dropping of all attachments. It is only when I cease to cling to you, to need you, to possess you that I can begin to love you . . . Love requires freedom, and freedom is lost in the attachment.'[16]

We look now at the ways in which Ignatius suggests God manifests his will.

Three ways for discernment

The first way is when we are, as it were, 'zapped'. The decision seems to come out of nowhere but we know for sure that it is the will of God. We know that we have been touched by God. David Hay's research into religious experience has already been quoted. One of his conclusions is that 36 per cent of the population have at some time been aware of or influenced by a presence or a power. Eighteen per cent have been influenced just once or twice.[17] A typical example of this kind is as follows:

It happened on a Sunday morning, the last day of a weekend retreat. Matthew had visited the chapel. As he knelt down he experienced a powerful shock – like a bolt of lightning. He felt his whole being lifted up. He had to say 'yes'. He had to enter the ministry. He had no control over it. All he could do was go with it. There were no arguments, no doubts. It was decided. There was total certainty that God has spoken. He experienced a great sense of peace, joy and direction. He knew he had been chosen by God.

One could argue that Matthew and Paul were called in this particular way. They had no doubts that God was calling them to follow him.

This is a depth of experience, which the soul cannot reach by its own efforts. It comes across as utterly convincing and compelling and carries with it a rightness that cannot be challenged. There is an absolute certainty and clarity around the choice. Of course there is the need to take the experience to God in prayer to gain confirmation.

It has to be said that discernment of God's will through this 'zapping' kind of experience does not happen very often in the lives of Christians. It is far more likely that the second or third types of discernment will apply. The second type, or time, to use Ignatian terminology, is very much based on the conviction that God communicates through our feelings. All discernment involves feelings but in this second time there is a special focus on our affective states and our cognitive processes are brought to bear to evaluate these feelings. In Ignatian terms this is his 'discernment of spirits' and this is about looking at a person's experience and noting the significant changes or movements in the feelings which are associated with a particular course of action or actions. Through those observations the hope is that one can discern the activity of God and the forces which may be resisting it.

The two words, which Ignatius frequently uses in this context, are 'consolation' and 'desolation'. Indeed this second time of discernment is 'when much light and understanding are derived through experience of desolations and consolations and discernment of diverse spirits' (#176). Ignatius' own definitions of consolation and desolation are given in the Exercises paragraphs 316–17. The feelings are to do with whether a person is experiencing a movement towards God or a movement away from God. In brief, consolation is the experience of being drawn closer to God so that we are less self-centred and more open to others. Typical feelings associated with this experience are joyful awareness, a sense of gratitude, a state of peace and so on. 'The main feature of them is that their direction is towards growth, creativity and a genuine fullness of life and love in that they draw us to a fuller, effective, generous love of God and other people, and to a right love of ourselves.'[18] These are pleasant feelings of joy, peace and delight in the love of God and being a disciple of Jesus. Sometimes these feelings seem to come, as it were, out of nowhere, and without any apparent cause.

> God alone can give consolation to the soul without any previous cause ... that is, without any preceding perception or knowledge of any subject by which a soul might be led to such a consolation through its own acts of intellect and will. (# 330)

This notwithstanding, there are all sorts of pitfalls into which one can fall. Feelings of consolation can be deceptive. It is part of our human nature to be resistant to the Spirit of God. 'It is characteristic of the Evil One to fight against such happiness and consolation by proposing fallacious reasoning, subtleties, and continual deceptions' (# 329). People can be led astray by apparent good. This is what Lonsdale calls 'the serpent's tail'.[19]

Ignatius gives rules which outline the dangers (# 329–36). For example, the fourth rule states 'it is a mark of the evil spirit to assume the appearance of an angel of light. He begins by suggesting thoughts that are suited to a devout soul, and ends by suggesting his own' (#333). One possible indication of this is that good suggestions are often far-fetched, for example, a newcomer to Christianity may be directed to organize a mission to Mongolia. A key test is whether the resulting decision draws the person away from Christ or closer to Christ. Even when there is consolation without previous cause there is need to carefully assess what follows in the after-glow. 'We must carefully assess the whole course of our thoughts and see if these thoughts are 'less good' or 'distracting' or 'terminate in something evil, or distracting, or less good than the soul had formerly proposed to do' (#332). These thoughts are the cognitive signs of a deceptive good.

A further test that Ignatius gives is that 'in souls that are progressing to greater perfection, the action of the good angel is delicate, gentle, delightful. It may be compared to a drop of water penetrating a sponge. The action of the evil spirit upon such souls is violent, noisy, and disturbing. It may be compared to a drop of water falling upon a stone' (#335). If the experience is producing great trouble, disturbance and turmoil rather than peace and tranquillity, serious questions have to be raised. This is the case where the deceptive good speaks to our feelings, that is, our affective experience.

Feelings of desolation are the complete opposite of those named above: restlessness, inner darkness, life ceases to have meaning, failure, guilt and so on. 'Their characteristic tendency is to draw us away from God and things which have to do with God, and lead us to be self-centred, closed in and unconcerned about God or other people.'[20] These are unpleasant feelings but are not necessarily destructive. Ignatius writes that these experiences can be occasions for growth if dealt with correctly (#318–22). However, it is very important that decisions are not made when we are in a time of desolation, precisely because such decisions could be destructive and lead us away from God (#318). For example, it is not usually a good idea to make a major decision when suffering a bereavement. Furthermore 'though in desolation we must never change our former resolutions' (#319). Indeed the suggestion is that we act against the desolation by intensifying our prayer, meditation and self-examination.

For example, Pat has been a church layworker for a number of years and her work is greatly valued. However, she has recently been asked about a ministry in the diaconate. She feels attracted to the presbyteral ministry and has the gifts necessary but wonders whether it is the right time. With the help of her spiritual director she tries to discern God's will for her by using this second mode of Ignatian discernment. She tries to discern her dispositions, whether they be attractions or aversions, when she considers before God her experiences as a layworker. She follows the same process when she considers the possibility of being a presbyteral minister. Time is spent in prayer trying to be indifferent to either position and seeking only to do God's will. The process of discernment is a matter of sifting through the various feelings and discovering those, which bring desolation, and those, which bring consolation.

The crucial question is not so much where feelings are coming from. To know this is the proper domain for counselling but for discernment the crucial question is in which direction the feelings are leading. What is the affective movement? Ignatius gives further rules for the discernment of spirits (#329–36) and especially highlights the fact that sometimes consolation can be false. Though good in themselves the experiences may be drawing us away from something better. In colourful language he compares the 'enemy . . . in his manner of acting to a false lover. He seeks to remain hidden and does not want to be discovered' (#326). In these cases Ignatius gives two pieces of advice. First, we must trace back from the harmful experience to the time when things started to go wrong (#333–34); and second, tell somebody what is happening (#326).

In summary this second type of discernment is to do with the critical evaluation of one's experience to see whether there are feelings of desolation or consolation at work. Because there is such a thing as false consolation, false joy and peace, a basic method of discernment is to note the final result. One thing to do is to examine the whole course of our thoughts. 'If the beginning and middle and end of the course of thoughts are wholly good and directed to what is entirely right, it is a sign that they are from the good angel' (#333). If the course of our thoughts terminates in something evil or something that causes a disturbance or disquiet this is a 'clear sign that the thoughts are proceeding from the evil spirit' (#333). 'The Christian must wait to discover where the inspiration leads, or where it has lead to in the past. Does it lead to humility or to pride, to looking beyond ourselves or into ourselves?'[21] Let it be said that although Ignatius focuses on the humility and poverty of Jesus 'he is not an advocate of beggary but a genuine promoter of Christian liberty',[22] and we move on in our spiritual lives in so far as we 'liberate ourselves from self-love, from our own will, and from our own interests'.[23]

The third time or mode of discernment is during a time of tranquillity 'a time when the soul is not agitated by different spirits, and has free and peaceful use of its natural powers' (#177). It takes place in the context of considering first the purpose for which we are born 'that is, for the praise of God our Lord and for the salvation of (our) soul' (#177). From this beginning Ignatius now gives two ways for determining a choice. The first way can seem to be very rational.

Basically it is to have in mind the object about which a choice is to be made and then listing all the advantages and disadvantages. However, it is not simply a question of the longest list which determines the outcome. Because I am 'like a balance at equilibrium, without leaning to either side'(#179), it is more a question of weighing up the pros and cons. This weighting process may lead a person to decide, for example, that one advantage may outweigh more than one disadvantage. 'Then I must come to a decision in the matter under deliberation because of the weightier motive presented to my reason, and not because of any sensual inclination' (#182).

At the end of the process the person has to go to God in prayer to seek confirmation of the decision, as, indeed, confirmation is required for all three kinds of choice. 'After such a choice or decision, the one who has made it must turn with great diligence to prayer in the presence of God our Lord, and offer Him his choice that the Divine Majesty may deign to accept and confirm it if it is for His greater service and praise' (#183). This confirmation comes not through a clinical analysis but by an affective experience of consolation or through the absence of disconfirmation. Confirmation could also come, after such an analysis, through the 'zapping' experience of the first method of discernment. It could also come by using the second way in the third method of discernment.

The second way in type three discernment uses the imagination. The person making the choice has to imagine telling a person they have never known what they have chosen for the greater glory of God. Or the person has to imagine they are on their deathbed. Would they still have made the same choice? Finally they have to imagine they are standing before their judge on the last day and again reflect on the decision they would have wished to have made (#185–87). As with the first process there has to be confirmation in the form of a feeling of consolation.

It is important to notice that all three modes of discernment not only necessitate a process of confirmation but they take place within a context of prayer. Prayer is actually part of the decision-making process. In the Exercises themselves what is called the Election actually takes place during the second week when the retreatant is contemplating the life of Christ. It is the life of Jesus that provides the focus for any choices that are made. During the second week the person is engaging in a discernment process but the life of Jesus is a reference point. This helps to ensure that the decision reached 'is coherent with and a concrete expression of our commitment to being disciples of Jesus'.[24]

In conclusion it can be seen that discernment lies at the heart of Ignatian spirituality. However, it also lies at the heart of all spirituality. In all our lives there are choices to be made. Some are more important than others and some decisions we make through prayerful consideration. Other decisions are more difficult to make because they involve fundamental changes to our way of life and however much we desire to do God's will it is often not apparent quite what God's will for us is. However, Ignatius in his Exercises gives three modes of making a choice. His rules in principle can be applied to any situation in which a mature Christian is genuinely seeking to discern God's will. They presuppose a background in which an individual is living a life in relationship to God and who is trying to be responsive to the promptings of the Holy Spirit.

However, following these rules does not imply that God has *a* will that we simply have to discover and put into effect. Ignatius' methods are much more flexible than the word 'rules' would imply. They are not about obeying an external law or, indeed, about doing anything. Supremely they are about listening and responding to what has been heard in the here and now. They are about being at one with God and being tuned in to him. Ignatius supplies us with the tools for discerning the voice of God through the movements of feelings within us – our consolations and desolations. Thus God's will is discerned for a particular individual in a particular set of circumstances. The 'right' decision is the best in the circumstances but the freer the individual is, the more detached, the more likely it is that God's desire will become clear and the more likely it is that the will of God will not appear as a 'merciless bully'.[25]

As we have seen no one is entirely free. We are all limited in one way or another. However, it could be argued that the very point of the Ignatian Exercises is to arrive at a point of greater interior freedom and a greater understanding of where we are not free. Indeed the Exercises close with the 'contemplation for attaining divine love' (## 230–37). 'What is needed is to have a free heart, and in this sense the contemplation for attaining love is the fruit of the entire journey of the Exercises.'[26] To the extent that we are able to free ourselves from all that binds us and holds us back, we are able to discern and enact God's will for us. What is certain is that whatever is God's plan for us, 'it is a safe bet that it will cut across any plans of our own'.[27]

9

Focusing on Jesus

As we have seen the focus for any process of discernment is the life of Jesus. It is there that we find our inspiration.

> Objectively speaking, no call comes from God to any person except in the person of Christ Jesus: and no person makes a response to God's call except in the person of Christ Jesus. This is only one way of expressing the fundamental biblical truth of Christ's unique mediation; 'there is one God; there is also one mediator between God and humankind, Christ Jesus himself human' (1 Timothy 2.5).[1]

The main thrust of the Exercises is for the retreatant to contemplate or focus on the life of Jesus as he appears in the four Gospels. 'Contemplative prayer, as we use the term here, means paying attention to and becoming at least slightly absorbed in the person of Jesus, in God or in biblical persons.'[2] At a very basic level the act of contemplating something or someone outside of oneself helps to free one of the internal distractions of which we spoke in an earlier chapter. Simply being absorbed, say, in a good book, or game of tennis, enables one to forget oneself. If our internal agenda is too great we cannot hope to contemplate prayerfully. If, for example, I am very tired or very thirsty, it may be helpful to meet these needs before attempting to contemplate anything, let alone the life of Jesus.

Ignatian prayer draws on an ancient way of reading

scripture that does not depend on bible study as such. This is called *lectio divina*.[3]

> *Lectio* looks to the bible as the genuine word of God, a privileged text by which Christians are continually nourished in faith ... *Lectio* is undertaken in the conviction that God's word is meant to be a good word ... It is an encounter with the living God. It is prayer.[4]

Ignatian prayer draws more fully on the use of the imagination.

Only by using our imagination can we really hope to understand what it was like to have sat at the feet of this wandering Jew from Nazareth. This is the Ignatian approach, to imagine actively that you are part of a particular biblical scene or story and to find where you yourself are in it.[5] Do you find yourself to be part of the crowd, an interested or disinterested bystander, one of the disciples, male or female and so on. To engage with Scripture at this level is to discover a rich seam of spiritual food. Of course, one could be criticized for using the Bible in a very subjective way but it does work. It is not using the Bible simply as a source of information or a collection of books that can be critically analyzed but it is using it as a source of spiritual life. This is a recognition of the fact that just as the events in the Gospels depict the action of God 2,000 years ago, supremely in the life of Jesus, so God is able to act and speak now through the lives of individuals as they imaginatively enter into those events today. Difficulties arise when people 'are so enamoured of the truth of history that they miss the truth of mystery. Truth for them is only historical, not mystical'.[6]

There follows a few personal examples of using this imaginative approach to Scripture and the life of Jesus, in particular. I had to try to listen to what the text was saying to me in the here and now. It will be noticed that I often had a clash between head and heart. This conflict between the brain and the heart was a constant theme throughout my 30 days. As we shall see, this conflict came to a head when the resurrection was contemplated.

The annunciation: Luke 1.26–38

We read that Mary was 'much perplexed'. No wonder! It is not everyday that someone appears to us to say that we are going to have a baby especially if we are not married. How many times have I been troubled by unexpected news or by events I could not make sense of? While ministering to a church in Scotland I developed with the congregation a scheme for a new building. The plans were quite well-advanced when I received a letter saying that another building was for sale and were we interested. This seemed a better proposition than building from scratch. We therefore changed our plans. However the purchase of the new building depended on the sale of the old building. We had a potential buyer but at the very last minute he pulled out. The plans had to be changed again. Never were the words of Burns so appropriate: 'The best laid schemes o' Mice an' Men, Gang aft agley'.[7]

Time can be spent on laying our plans and deciding what we want to do. Everything that subsequently happens has to fit into our timetable and our convenience. In this way God is excluded. The wonderful thing about Mary is that although she was troubled and although the possibility of a pregnancy was, no doubt, very inconvenient, she was obedient. 'Here am I, the servant of the Lord; let it be with me according to your word.' I have attended many, many ecumenical meetings where a discussion has taken place about the possibility of a United Service, say, on Good Friday. This has often been extraordinarily difficult simply because the representatives of each church say that they always have a service at a particular time. In other words to do something different does not fit in with their plans. Thus God is squeezed out and onto the cross. To celebrate

Easter Sunday in an ecumenical gathering is even more difficult.

It is important to note that Mary's response was in the context of consolation. 'Do not be afraid' was the response of the angel to her agitation. We shall see that the Risen Lord also gives great consolation to those to whom he appears. The important thing here is that Mary listens to the word of God. She opened herself and became vulnerable. Instead of becoming defensive and making up all kinds of excuses her only desire was to do what God wanted. Presumably she had no idea as to the significance or the implications of what was asked of her. How could she? My aim on the retreat became more and more that of listening to God and finding out what he was asking of me while at the same time having no idea at all where it would all lead. It became a matter of complete trust. 'For nothing will be impossible with God.'

The birth of Jesus: Luke 2.1–7

What a daring risk for God to take on human form. He becomes totally vulnerable and dependent on other human beings, us. We can all identify with a baby. Even in this secular world Christmas still holds a great attraction. Churches are fuller at Christmas than at any other time of the year. This ancient story seems to speak to people at a very deep level, perhaps because babies are not threatening. They are not going to harm us in any meaningful way. Furthermore we can more easily lose our inhibitions with a baby and become childlike ourselves. We gaze and coo at babies and play with them and do things that we would not normally dream of doing.

Yet even here God was shut out. 'There was no place for them in the inn.' Even pregnant women and babies can be marginalized. We are all quite adept at projecting our innermost fears on to other people. It is often those on the margins of society who are the recipients of our projections. They then appear to threaten us and so we shut them out. The reality is that the fears are within us. If we let Jesus in what will he find and what will happen to us? Will our fears be assuaged or will we become more uncomfortable? There is likely to be a degree of discomfort to say the least if we really let Jesus in. Some births are easier than others but most have a long labour and all have a roughly equal length of gestation.

At one level this passage obviously speaks of the astounding fact of God becoming man in the birth of Jesus. However at a much deeper level it spoke to my vulnerability or lack of it and to my dependence or lack of it. It also spoke to my obedience or lack of it. Finally there was the need to look after my 'child'. We all have a 'child' dimension within us and this needs to be nourished and cared for. There needs to be time for creativity, fun and enjoyment in life.

King Herod: Matthew 2

Presumably, like all kings, Herod was a man of authority. He was secure, powerful, independent and leading a steady, predictable kind of life. How many of these descriptions applied to me? The threat to Herod was immense when he heard that another king had been born. Am I going to feel threatened by the birth of Jesus? What is it going to mean to me? Is he going to usurp my authority and independence? Do I want to search him out and kill him, if not literally, then metaphorically? In what ways do I kill Jesus everyday because he poses a threat to my way of life and to my security? His very existence is a threat to my comfortable, middle-class way of life.

It became necessary at this point to accept the guidance of Ignatius and enter upon a colloquy, a dialogue with God:

'Will I lose my authority?'
'You will have mine.'

'Will I lose my independence?'
'Yes, you must learn to depend on me.'
'Will I feel threatened?'
'All I want is your well-being. I mean you no harm.'

Could all this be true? It certainly seemed safer to analyze the texts and apply the methods of biblical criticism and the tools of historical research. This kind of approach to Scripture is challenging me in ways hitherto unknown.

Simeon and Anna: Luke 2:25–38

I have been regularly and faithfully attending the temple. The Faith and the community of faith are very important to me. I had a premonition that something important was going to happen. I went to the temple and immediately I saw what I had been waiting for throughout my life. A baby had been brought in by his parents and I just knew that this was the Christ, the Messiah who would be 'a light for revelation to the Gentiles'. With what joy I took that baby in my arms and gave thanks to God. Now I know what I have been waiting for all this time. I cannot say how I knew. Intuitively it was quite obvious.

My intuition was confirmed by the prophetess Anna. She had been around the temple for years and years. Nobody knew quite how old she was. She seemed to lead a very odd kind of life because she never left the temple. However, because of her constant prayers and fasting it was clear to all who met her that she was very close to God. Anna confirmed my conviction. Without any discussion on the matter she gave thanks to God for the child and 'spoke of him to all who were looking for the redemption of Jerusalem'. People began to gather round.

Of course there are many questions that could be asked. However it seems that some things have to be taken on trust. Simeon and Anna asked no questions at all. They were absolutely sure who the baby was.

The baptism of Jesus: Matthew 3.13–17

One of the great understatements of the Gospels is the fact
of Jesus leaving home. Was his father disappointed that he
was not carrying on the family business? Was his mother
upset that he was just leaving home without any apparent
destination? Clearly he was old enough to know his own
mind but was he mad or did he have a plan of his
intentions? The whole incident must have been quite
traumatic. It wasn't as though he was going off to college
or university or the equivalent that would have been to
study as a rabbi at the temple in Jerusalem. Jesus must have
had a very strong sense of vocation, a sense that God was
guiding him. This becomes apparent at his baptism. 'This
is my Son, the Beloved, with whom I am well pleased.'

Again, all kinds of questions could be asked. Why was it
necessary for Jesus to be baptized at all? Tradition says he
was sinless. Certainly there is no suggestion in the Gospels
that he was one of the bad guys of the neighbourhood.
How could he then die to sin and be raised to new life? My
feelings during this meditation revealed a great sense of
identity with Jesus. He demonstrated his identity with
humanity and his dependence on God by being baptized. It
is this baptism which also unites Christians to each other.
This identity which transcends all barriers is not
automatic. Many parents have their children 'done' and
are not part of the fellowship of believers. The seed that is
planted at baptism has to grow. In other words, with
baptism there has to be an increasing sense of responsibility.

The temptations: Matthew 4.1–11

Again there were lots of questions. Why was Jesus 'driven
by the Spirit'? Did he really spend 40 days in the wilderness
or is the number 40 simply a biblical metaphor for a long
time? Did he spend all the time fasting? How do we know

what the temptations were since, temptations are, by definition internal events? Furthermore we are only tempted to do the things which are possible. Could Jesus really have turned stones into bread and been saved by angels if he had thrown himself off the pinnacle of the temple? Is there such a being as the devil and did he really speak to Jesus?

To begin to answer these questions would have again been to miss the point. We have all had the experience of being tempted. Those occasions that draw us away from God and that, when we succumb to them, are usually destructive either for our own well being or the well being of others. They often lead to courses of action, which then lead on to increasing our status, authority or popularity. It is not necessary to postulate whether there is a devil or not. We are all too conscious of the presence and the power of evil within ourselves and within the world. 'We blame the Devil for the Evil we do, and for the Evil we tolerate, and for the Evil we do not prevent, and which we dare not condemn.'[8] 'The evil powers are in Man, in his own nature, in the very nature of his self-love, his egotism, his ignorance, his stupidity, his malice, his vanity . . . these defects are collectively called the *Devil*.'[9]

The power of the temptations for Jesus was remarkable; to feed himself and the hungry, to demonstrate the power of God and to exert his authority over others. These were surely all desirable aims. They offer things that appear to be good and reasonable. We might call these temptations today sensual enjoyment, power over the elements and power over others. Jesus overcomes these with great inner strength. They are the right aims but the wrong methods. They are based on power, status and instant recognition and thereby take away people's freedom to choose for themselves. Jesus overcomes the temptations by submitting to the will of God and distinguishing between what is creative and what is destructive. Inner development is only possible in times of trial, or suffering, or temptation. We do not grow inwardly when things are going well.

How many times have I felt myself to be in the wilderness? These are the occasions when we are unsure which way to turn. The road ahead is not clearly marked. The temptation is to follow our own ideas and depend on our own resources. How many times do I give in to temptation in order to be popular and avoid conflict? Yet Jesus does not do the crowd-pleasing thing. I felt a great deal of encouragement in my temptations in the knowledge that Jesus had overcome the subtlest temptations. He knows what it is like to be tested. I felt he would be with me in my trials and supply me with the necessary inner strength. He understands.

The call of the disciples: Luke 5.1–11

Simon, Peter, James and John had been out fishing all night and caught nothing. Jesus told them to go out again and they caught a great shoal of fish. The fishermen were astonished and Peter, in particular, was quite overcome. 'And when they had brought their boats to shore, they left everything and followed him.' This is another good example of understatement in the Gospels. What happened to all the fish they had caught? What about their boats? Didn't they want to say good-bye to their families and pack up some spare clothes? Peter has the reputation of being very practical and down-to-earth. Did he leave everything just like that and follow this person whom he had not met before?

Jesus seems to have the most extraordinary authority. He speaks and acts with such power. He has the capacity to inspire people and draw them to himself. It is a kind of magnetism. He creates such great anticipation and expectancy in people that they want to give up everything to follow him. It is like selling everything to buy a field in which there is buried treasure.

Have I been 'out fishing' during my ministry and not caught very much? Perhaps I need to stop concentrating on what I am doing and try to discern what God is doing. This needs a different kind of attentiveness. I am willing to follow Jesus and try to do so but am I willing to give up anything or do I try to hang on to my possessions? Where is the sense of anticipation and expectancy in my ministry? Have I forgotten how to attempt great things for God and expect great things from him? Yet he is the God of surprises. Perhaps he is waiting to fill my 'nets' with a great shoal of fish. After all God cannot be outdone in generosity. 'Give, and it will be given to you; good measure, pressed down, shaken together, running over, will be put into your lap' (Luke 6.38).

Walking on water: Matthew 14.22–23

This was a crunch passage. Did Jesus really walk on water? If he did that raises all kinds of questions about the activity of God in the world today. If Jesus has control over the elements, why doesn't God intervene today and control earthquakes, hurricanes and such like? Furthermore if Jesus walks on water he clearly is divine. Where does that leave his humanity? It is important for me that Jesus is entirely human and not simply God dressed up in a human guise. Of course it could be that the 'sea' is symbolic, as it often is in the Old Testament, for evil and dark forces. The passage then is about the power of Jesus over these forces. I began to 'feel' myself into the passage.

Whether this incident happened in a literal sense or not is of no importance. What is significant is the times in my life I have felt myself to be sinking. When the ground has not felt very secure under my feet. When my life has been going through rough waters and I have begun to lose my bearings. When I have been beset by fears about the future. As with Peter the cry is 'Lord, save me.' Jesus immediately reached out his hand and caught him and said, 'You of little faith, why did you doubt?' There is the power, the significance. Jesus is always there even if we are not always aware of it. We have to let God be God and Jesus be Jesus. Only then can we truly 'fear not'.

The transfiguration: Matthew 17.1–8

For reasons I found it hard to discover I did not want to go up the mountain with Jesus. I was very reluctant. It seemed so unnecessary to go for a long, hard climb when there was plenty of work to do. However, I was eventually persuaded. It seemed to be a very special occasion because Jesus only took Peter, James and John. There was not much talking on the way but we eventually reached the summit, tired and breathless. The view was awe-inspiring; the snow-capped peaks in front of us and the valley in the distance below. We were soaking up the view when suddenly Jesus seemed to change. Not only that, he appeared to be talking to Moses and Elijah. Like most people who climb mountains and throw a stone on the cairn at the top we also wanted to mark the spot especially as this event was so magnificent and so unique. We all seemed to gain the insight together that Jesus was greater than either of these two great heroes of the Old Testament. In fact we distinctly heard a voice saying, 'This is my son, the beloved with whom I am well pleased; listen to him.' Instinctively we fell on our knees. We were full of fear but Jesus said, 'Get up and do not be afraid.'

Perhaps this was the reason for my reluctance in the first place. We had seen the reality of Jesus. In other words we had seen his glory. We had seen who he really was. The reality was overwhelming. It also carries amazing implications. If Jesus is truly the Son of God, then I have to listen to what he has to say to me.

These have been a few selected incidents from the life of Jesus. I have attempted to use the Ignatian technique of praying into the various events to see where I am in them and what they are saying to me. This was often a great effort since I had to overcome my natural desire to use my intellect and ask all sorts of questions about the text. This conflict which might be described as a battle between the head and the heart came to a climax when the resurrection of Jesus was considered.

The resurrection

What *really* happened at that first Easter? Why is it that sometimes Jesus was clearly recognized while at other times he was not? Sometimes the accounts suggest that the risen Lord could be physically seen and touched, indeed, he eats breakfast with the disciples, while at other times he passes through locked doors or simply disappears from sight. Was the resurrection, therefore, something physical or something spiritual? Clearly there is a difference between resuscitation and resurrection but what was the precise nature of the resurrection? Does the empty tomb have any significance, since Paul does not mention it at all? In fact Mark's Gospel says very little about the resurrection, just that the tomb was empty.[10] Does the risen Lord continue to appear to his followers today or did the appearances finish after the ascension? If they did, how do we describe Paul's experience on the Damascus Road? If we are to be intellectually honest, the resurrection poses many, many questions. However, in true Ignatian fashion I tried to follow the promptings of my heart as I meditated during the final week. Would God have some more surprises in store?

The women at the tomb: Mark 16.1–8

I went with Mary Magdalene and Mary the mother of James, and Salome to the tomb as soon as the Sabbath was over. They were taking spices in order to anoint the body.

It was a very sombre kind of walk. No one said a word. We just wondered who was going to roll the stone away. When we got to the tomb we were absolutely amazed to find that the stone had already been rolled away. Was this the right tomb? Where was the body?. Had someone stolen it? 'Where are you, Lord?' The reply came back, 'With you', but it was said in almost a condescending kind of way as if to say, 'What a stupid question!' I was left with a feeling of total disbelief. We didn't say anything to anyone we were so unsure about what had happened. In fact we didn't know what had happened.

The road to Emmaus: Luke 24.13–35

This was a very strange journey. We were talking to each other about the events of the last few days and trying to make sense of them. We didn't get very far. All we knew for certain was that our friend and leader had been crucified and buried in a tomb. A stranger joined us on the way who didn't seem to have the faintest idea what we were talking about. It was as though he had been living in a different world. The remarkable thing is that he knew the Jewish Scriptures like the back of his hand. He told us all about Moses and the prophets. He even said it was necessary for Christ to suffer and enter his glory. The journey went very quickly.

As evening approached we arrived at our destination, the village of Emmaus. The stranger wanted to go on but we constrained him to join us for supper and spend the night with us. As we began to eat something quite incredible happened. The stranger took the bread and blessed it. He then broke it and gave some to each of us. Then, at that precise moment my eyes were opened. I knew who the stranger was. Before I could say anything he just vanished out of sight.

I remembered what he had said earlier, 'O how foolish you are, and slow of heart to believe.' This was me, *slow of heart* to believe. I then had an experience of pure, unadulterated peace and consolation. There was a distinct presence in the room, almost tangible enough to touch. This could only be described as a resurrection appearance in the here and now. To that extent the text no longer became important.

It can be seen that this overwhelming experience did not happen immediately. But this, it seems to me, is true to life. As we know experiences of pain, suffering and bereavement are not overcome in two days and, to state the obvious, death is a necessary precursor for any experience of new life. Perhaps that is why Jesus related the parable about the grain of wheat, finding in it a truth for himself as well as for those who were to follow his example. 'Unless a grain of wheat falls into the earth and dies, it remains just a single grain; but if it dies, it bears much fruit' (John 12.24). However the process of bereavement is a process which has been well-documented and all we can do very often is simply 'stay with it' knowing that God is with us and waiting to work out his purposes. In the Bible the gap between Good Friday and Easter Sunday is very small. In reality it is much longer. Furthermore the experience of new life is, for some, a gradual kind of understanding while for others it is much more dramatic.

I was not deliberately looking for any kind of dramatic experience. Far from it. If the truth be known my natural scepticism was predominant. I am not an overtly emotional kind of person and am a little suspicious of those who seem to require instant spirituality or need 'spiritual kicks' in order to sustain their Christian commitment. This, to me, is a phoney kind of religion and smacks of superficiality. It demonstrates a lack of faith rather than a deep commitment to the Way of the Cross.

The experience was not one that induced fear. Quite the reverse. Indeed in most of the biblical appearances Jesus often utters words of consolation 'Do not be afraid.' My experience entirely corroborated this. Of course I had known it with my head but now it was a different kind of knowledge. It was in the heart. For this to happen I had to let go of my cerebral control and let God be God. This can be a bit unnerving at first but the rewards are beyond words.

Jesus appears in the upper room: John 20.19–30

I was very restless during this session and there were all sorts of distractions. There was a certain amount of tiredness but this was not the cause of the restlessness. It was more a feeling of uneasiness. My eyes were attracted to the words, 'he breathed on them, and said to them, "Receive the Holy Spirit".' Herein lay the roots of my inner disturbance. I was afraid. The last thing I wanted was some dramatic expression of the gift of the Spirit. Speaking in tongues, for example, has always seemed to be of dubious value. Under the appropriate conditions people can be induced to do all manner of things which are not necessarily manifestations of the presence of the Spirit. I am quite sure that not all spiritual experiences are from God. Furthermore it is a spirituality which has very little, if anything, to do with the needs of my neighbour. Moreover people who have this experience all too readily fall into the trap of worshipping the experience itself rather than the experience of God.

My desire was for something much less dramatic and yet at the same time much more costly. I requested the gift of love. I want 'to love others as you have loved us'. The reply was instantaneous. 'You shall have it.' Now I experienced that peace which is beyond all human understanding.

There is a danger here. God longs to show himself to us but this can only happen when we become open and receptive. In effect we have to say 'yes' to God. Then he can disturb us in a profound, but gentle way. Loving and being loved always involves a risk. Loving God is one side of the coin; being loved by him is another. This is the danger.

Who knows what might happen if we allow ourselves to be loved by God?

The sea of Tiberias: John 21.1–14

This passage reminded me of an earlier one that I had meditated on at the time of the call of the disciples. Was this the same event which this writer had put in a different place for theological reasons? Is there any significance in being told to cast the net on the 'right' side of the boat? Do fishermen usually bother to count their catch? What was the meaning, if any, of the number 153? Was the resurrection of Jesus so physical that he was able to cook breakfast? Do we have this description in the Fourth Gospel because it is the last of the Gospels to be written and the appearances become progressively more physical?

All of these questions are clearly questions for the head and answers, or at least, interpretations and suggestions can be obtained from commentaries. At this point in time they had no importance. My heart said quite clearly with the disciple whom Jesus loved 'It is the Lord!' In fact all the disciples 'knew it was the Lord'. They recognized this figure by the lake as the same as the earthly Jesus they had known and shared their lives with. Yet somehow he was different. How this could be I did not know. It did not matter. Above all else this kind of contemplative exercise is about learning to see.

On the mountain: Matthew 28.16–20

These verses are the last in the Gospel. I have often wondered about the fact that among the group of people present 'some doubted'. In spite of having seen Jesus and witnessed some of the things he had said and done, they still retained their hesitations. I took comfort from this in that I also still had doubts. However, when I began to meditate on the passage a strange thing happened. To my surprise I found myself on the side of the believers. Now quite clearly, with my heart, I was on the other side of the fence trying to convince the doubters that Jesus indeed was who he said he was, the Son of God. I felt myself almost bursting to tell others. 'Go therefore and make disciples of all nations.'

My retreat had taken me to the top of the mountain and I had seen the risen Lord. I had seen with my own eyes and experienced with my own heart. I went again on the walk I had taken 30 days before. I saw again the empty farmhouse still looking very sturdy and well-built, but quite empty. It did not speak to me at all. I walked a few yards further. Another house came into view. This also looked very interesting. I wanted to go in and look around. This was the building that spoke to me. It was lived in.

I have preached on the theme of the resurrection many times. I have read the commentaries and tried to make sense of it. I have even said that the important thing about the event is not what happened 2,000 years ago, but what happens in the here and now. To look for the precise answers to the questions posed at the beginning of this chapter can only throw a certain amount of light on to the mystery. However it is to concentrate on the chrysalis rather than the butterfly. St Francis once likened the resurrection to a lark soaring in the skies, a symbol of freedom and celebration. Now the freedom and the celebration are a part of me. The resurrection experience has become interior knowledge – a knowledge that can only be appropriated through faith and never through the medium of historical investigation. But it is a new kind of knowledge that arises out of the historical message. In an Ignatian sense, this is getting a taste and feel for the truth. What this encounter means for the future is an open question. God, will no doubt, have many more surprises.

To the contemporary world of strife, violence, tension,

suffering and anxiety,
both the circus and Christianity present a view of a
wholly different kind of world:
not one of business as usual . . .
not things as they always have been . . .
not a world of ruts . . .

but a world
of surprise and delight . . .
a world of new possibilities . . .
a world of hope, of joy,
even in dark times . . .
a world that's unpredictable . . .
a world where all participate where no one's
left out – even the fool . . .
a world in which the unexpected and the
unprecedented can happen . . .
a world of celebration of all life . . .
a world of laughter as well as tears . . .
a world
that
celebrates
EASTER[11]

Not the man from Siam

From my viewpoint the whole of the retreat had been unpredictable. This is an aspect which although central to the Christian life is often forgotten. It is also central to the work of the clown. There is always the element of the unexpected in the clown's performance. 'The clown exposes the rebel in all of us who would oppose the system, break the rules, violate the taboos, strike out for freedom from repressive, suffocating, narrow little formulas for living.'[1] Quite a different experience from the Siamese gentleman of limerick fame:

> There once was a man from Siam
> Who said, 'Now I see what I am,
> Just a being that moves
> In predestinate grooves,
> Not a bus, not a car, but a tram!'[2]

This was the precise opposite of my retreat. I was definitely not a tram moving along in defined ways. In no way could I have predicted what the outcome was going to be. Yet we speak glibly about our plans and God's plans for us. Where does that leave room for the movements of the Spirit, let alone the exercise of free will? 'The transcendent rarely goes by the rules. One has only to think of Jesus' entrance into this world to illustrate this. The entrance broke the accepted pattern. So did his exit, and his parables, and his life-style, and so on.'[3]

It feels as if I have travelled through the looking glass.

The world of the looking glass is where the laws of rational thought no longer seem to apply, where everything seems to be different and upside down and the laws of logic no longer appropriate. On one occasion Alice decides that she would like to meet the Red Queen.

> 'I think I'll go and meet her,' said Alice, for, though the flowers were interesting enough, she felt it would be far grander to have a talk with a real Queen.
> 'You can't possibly do that,' said the Rose. 'I should advise you to walk the other way.'
> This sounded nonsense to Alice, so she said nothing and set off at once towards the Red Queen. To her surprise she lost sight of her in a moment, and found herself walking in at the front-door again.
> A little provoked, she drew back, and, after looking everywhere for the Queen (whom she spied at last, a long way off), she thought she would try the plan, this time, of walking in the opposite direction.
> It succeeded beautifully. She had not been walking a minute before she found herself face to face with the Red Queen, and full in sight of the hill she had been so long aiming at.[4]

What a foolish thing to do, to walk in the opposite direction to where you want to go! The God of surprises invites us into his kingdom, but it is often not by the most obvious route. All the words in the world find God and his ways a mystery difficult to fathom but the heart has its own way of understanding. Dare we accept God's invitation to follow the foolishness of the cross?

Notes

Introduction

1 For many the thought of a 30-day retreat is simply not a viable possibility. However Ignatius takes account of this in what is called the 19th annotation or the Exercises in Daily Life. This simply means that retreatants are able to follow the pattern of the Exercises while still engaging in their daily life and work. They must, however, commit themselves to a daily pattern of about an hour for prayer and reflection. This way of following the Exercises, of course, is not restricted to 30 days. The process can take up to a year or longer.

2 Interestingly it has been said that 'Wesley was a kind of latter day Ignatius Loyola with his insistence on personal holiness, on discipline and "method" and on meditation on the Scriptures'. Kenneth Leech, *The Eye of the Storm*, Darton, Longman and Todd 1992, p. 27.

Chapter 1

1 K. Barth, *The Humanity of God*, Fontana 1967, pp. 12ff.

2 H. Zahrnt, *The Question of God*, Collins 1969, pp. 16f.

3 For a very good exposition of the relevance of biblical faith in the present world see: R. Richard Middleton and Brian J. Walsh, *Truth is Stranger than it Used to Be: Biblical Faith in a Post-Modern Age*, SPCK 1997.

4 Arthur R. Baranowski, *Creating Small Church Communities*, St Anthony Messenger Press, Cincinnati, Ohio 1996. New Way Publications provides resources for promoting a new way of being the church through small community formation (New Way Publications, Lodge Farmhouse, Groton, Sudbury, Suffolk).

5 John Drane, *The McDonaldization of the Church*, Darton, Longman and Todd 2000, p. 156.

6 Paul Lakeland, *Postmodernity, Christian Identity in a Fragmented Age*, Fortress Press, Minneapolis 1997, p. 49.

7 John Shelby Spong, *Why Christianity Must Change or Die*, Harper and Row 1998.

8 G.B. Caird, *Saint Luke*, The Pelican New Testament Commentaries 1971, p. 104.

9 # indicates the appropriate paragraph in Louis J. Puhl, *The Spiritual Exercises of Ignatius Loyola*, Loyola University Press 1951; ## indicates the appropriate paragraph in George E. Ganss, *Ignatius of Loyola, Spiritual Exercises and Selected Works*, The Classics of Western Spirituality, Paulist Press 1991.

10 Margaret Silf, *Landmarks: An Ignatian Journey*, Darton, Longman and Todd 1998, p. 73.

11 P. Sheldrake (ed.), *The Way of Ignatius Loyola*, SPCK 1991, p. 42.

12 Sheldrake, *The Way of Ignatius Loyola*, p. 17.

13 Sheldrake, *The Way of Ignatius Loyola*, p. 18.

14 It is very Ignatian to say that God is in every part of life. See for example, Margaret Hebblethwaite, *Finding God in All Things*, Fount 1994.

15 A few years later I went on this very same walk. The house was still there but although the frontage remained the same the interior was in the process of being completely rebuilt. In a similar way I felt that my spiritual interior had been completely rebuilt since the retreat.

16 Quoted in C.S. Lewis, *Daily Readings*, Fount 1992, p. 19.

Chapter 2

1 Neville J. Ward, *The Use of Praying*, Epworth 1967, p. 127.

2 Denis Duncan, *Creative Silence*, Arthur James Ltd 1980, p. 15.

3 John Carden, *Morning, Noon and Night*, Church Missionary Society 1976, p. 18.

4 Rubem A. Alves, *The Poet, the Warrior, the Prophet*, SCM Press 1990, p. 25.

5 Michel Quoist, *Prayers of Life*, Gill and Macmillan 1963, p. 15.

6 Hans Urs von Balthasar, *On Prayer*, SPCK 1973, p. 12. For Balthasar, God's word is ultimately himself or his son whom he sent into the world. 'The contemplation of scripture is the school where we learn to hear aright; there we make contact with the primary source of Christian life and prayer' (*On Prayer*, p. 26).

7 Hubert Richards, *What Happens When You Pray?*, SCM Press 1980, p. 34.

8 Petru Dumitriu, *To the Unknown God*, Collins 1982, p. 103.

9 von Balthasar, *On Prayer*, p. 27.

10 Thomas Merton, *Contemplative Prayer*, Darton, Longman and Todd 1973, p. 33.
11 Thomas Merton, *The Wisdom of the Desert*, Sheldon Press 1974, p.74.
12 Merton, *The Wisdom of the Desert* p. 55.
13 Thomas à Kempis, *On the Imitation of Christ*, Henry Frowde and Longmans, Green and Co. 1892, p. 29.
14 Julian of Norwich, *Revelations of Divine Love*, Penguin Classics 1966, p. 161.
15 Alan Jones, *Soul Making*, SCM Press 1985, p. 62.
16 Alves, *The Poet . . .* , p. 52.
17 T.S. Eliot, *Four Quartets*, Faber and Faber 1959, p. 27.
18 *Hymns and Psalms* 673.
19 St Teresa of Avila, *The Way of Perfection*, Joseph Leighton, Edinburgh 1942, pp. 149–50.
20 H. Backhouse (ed.), *The Dark Night of the Soul*, Hodder and Stoughton 1988, p. 32.
21 Merton, *Contemplative Prayer*, p. 103.
22 Merton, *Contemplative Prayer*, p. 112.
23 Gerard W. Hughes, *O God, Why?*, The Bible Reading Fellowship 1993, p. 32.
24 von Balthasar, *On Prayer*, p. 51.
25 von Balthasar, *On Prayer*, p. 63.
26 Julian of Norwich, *A Shewing of God's Love*, ed. Anna Maria Reynolds, Longman, Green and Co. Ltd 1974, p. 58.
27 Julian of Norwich, *A Shewing of God's Love*, p. 57.
28 Thomas Merton, *The Hidden Ground of Love*, Farrar, Straus, Giroux 1985, p. 158.
29 Merton, *Contemplative Prayer*, p. 115.
30 Simone Weil, *Waiting on God*, Fontana Religious 1959, p. 66.
31 Ward, *The Use of Praying*, p. 36.
32 Backhouse, *The Dark Night of the Soul*, p. 98.
33 Hughes, *O God, Why?*, p. 33.
34 St. Teresa of Arila, The *Way of Perfection*, p. 87.
35 Dumitriu, *To the Unknown God*, p. 84.
36 Robert M. Pirsig, *Zen and the Art of Motorcycle Maintenance*, Corgi 1984, p. 206.
37 *Hymns and Psalms* 354.
38 Anthony de Mello, *Awareness*, Fount 1990, p. 114.
39 J.-P. de Caussade, *The Sacrament of the Present Moment*, Collins 1981, p. 31.
40 de Caussade, *The Sacrament of the Present Moment*, p. 82.
41 de Caussade, *The Sacrament of the Present Moment*, p. 101.
42 Anthony de Mello, *The Song of the Bird*, Image Books 1984, p. 21.

43   Peter G. Jarvis, *Come to Terms*, Epworth 1979, p. 57.
44   P. Sheldrake (ed.), *The Way of Ignatius Loyola*, SPCK 1991, p. 22.
45   Gerard W. Hughes, *God of Surprises*, Darton, Longman and Todd
     1985, p. 31.

Chapter 3

 1   T. Waite, *Taken on Trust*, Hodder and Stoughton 1993.
 2   B. Keenan, *An Evil Cradling*, Vintage 1992.
 3   Petru Dumitriu, *To the Unknown God*, Collins 1982, p. 241.
 4   *Hymns and Psalms* 746.
 5   George Lovell, *An Experience of the Ignatian Exercises*, Epworth
     Review, vol. 21, no. 3 September 1994.
 6   Dumitriu, *To the Unknown God*, p. 27. This book has a powerful
     chapter on the nature of evil.
 7   Gerard W. Hughes, *O God, Why?*, The Bible Reading Fellowship
     1993, p. 65.
 8   Gerard W. Hughes, *God of Surprises*, Darton, Longman and Todd
     1985.

Chapter 4

 1   W.E. Sangster, *Methodism Can Be Born Again*, Hodder and
     Stoughton,1938.
 2   Sangster, *Methodism*, p. 25.
 3   Sangster, *Methodism*, p. 22.
 4   Rob Frost, *Which Way for the Church?*, Kingsway Publications
     1997, p. 56.
 5   Philip Francis and Leslie J. Richter, *Gone but not Forgotten*,
     Darton, Longman and Todd 1998, p. 59.
 6   James Redfield, *The Celestine Prophecy*, Bantam 1994.
 7   David Hay, *Exploring Inner Space*, Penguin 1982.
 8   David Hay, *A Source of Embarrassment?*, Transmission (Bible
     Society) Summer 1998, p. 3.
 9   David Hay, *Religion Lacking Spirit*, The Tablet, 2 March 1996,
     p. 292.
10   Simon Bailey, *The Well Within*, Darton, Longman and Todd 1996,
     p. 55.
11   Quoted in Albert Jewell (ed.), *Spirituality and Ageing*, Jessica
     Kingsley 1999, p. 10.
12   Diarmuid Ó Murchú, *Reclaiming Spirituality*, Gill and Macmillan
     1997, p. 31.
13   Source unknown.

14 Robert Towler, *The Need for Certainty*, Routledge and Kegan Paul 1984.

15 Towler, *The Need for Certainty*, p. 107.

16 Gerard W. Hughes, *God, Where Are You?*, Darton, Longman and Todd 1997, p. 264.

17 Sangster, *Methodism*, p. 33.

18 Hughes, *God, Where Are You?*, p. 90.

19 Gerard W. Hughes, *O God, Why?*, The Bible Reading Fellowship 1993, p. 23. The gist of the argument is that if we are really in favour of nuclear deterrence then our prayers should take the form of inspiring our scientists to invent more lethal weapons, and our economy so that we can purchase more of them.

20 Hughes, *O God, Why?*, p. 91. See Luke 16.19–31 for the story of the rich man and Lazarus.

21 Margaret Hebblethwaite, *Finding God in All Things*, Fount 1994, p. 14.

22 Francis Thompson, *The Kingdom of God* in *The Penguin Book of Religious Verse*, Penguin 1963, p. 45.

23 George E. Ganss, *Ignatius of Loyola, Spiritual Exercises and Selected Works*, The Classics of Western Spirituality, Paulist Press 1991, p. 130

24 Carl R. Rogers, *On Becoming a Person*, Constable 1988, pp. 22–3.

25 Rogers, *On Becoming a Person*, pp. 22–3.

Chapter 5

1 Charles Dickens, *Hard Times*, Oxford University Press 1987, p. 1.

2 Dickens, *Hard Times*, p. 5.

3 Gerard W. Hughes, *God of Surprises*, Darton, Longman and Todd 1985, p. 48.

4 James W. Fowler, *Becoming Adult, Becoming Christian*, Harper and Row 1984; and *Stages of Faith*, Harper and Row 1981.

5 Fowler, *Becoming Adult, Becoming Christian*, p. 65.

6 Anthony Storr, *The Integrity of the Personality*, Penguin 1963, p. 43.

7 Storr, *The Integrity of the Personality*, p. 43.

8 Storr, *The Integrity of the Personality*, p. 43.

9 Anthony Storr, *Human Aggression*, Penguin 1968, p. 87.

10 Dorothy Rowe, *Depression, The Way Out of Your Prison*, Routledge and Kegan Paul 1983.

11 John A. Sanford, *Ministry Burnout*, Arthur James Ltd 1982, see the chapter on 'The problem of the endless task'.

12 Jack Dominian, *The Capacity to Love*, Darton, Longman and Todd 1985, p. 149.
13 Thomas A. Harris, *I'm OK – You're OK*, Pan 1973, p. 25.
14 Harris, *I'm OK*, p. 44.
15 Harris, *I'm OK*, p. 44.
16 Storr, *Human Aggression*, p. 111.
17 Storr, *Human Aggression*, p. 67.
18 Kenneth Slack, *The Seven Deadly Sins*, SCM Press 1985, p. 74.
19 Konrad Lorenz, *On Aggression*, Methuen University Paperback 1979.
20 Paul Tournier, *The Violence Inside*, SCM Press 1978, p. 7.
21 Dorothy Rowe, *Depression: The Way Out of Your Prison*, Routledge and Kegan Paul 1983.
22 Robin Skynner and John Cleese, *Families and How to Survive Them*, Methuen 1983.
23 John Bowlby, *The Making and Breaking of Affectional Bonds*, Tavistock 1979.
24 David and Vera Mace, *Love and Anger in Marriage*, Pickering and Inglis 1983, p. 24.
25 Mace, *Love and Anger in Marriage*, p. 15.
26 Alastair V. Campbell, *The Gospel of Anger*, SPCK 1986.
27 Gerard W. Hughes, *God, Where Are You?*, Darton, Longman and Todd 1997, p. 149.
28 Hughes, *God, Where Are You?*, p. 151.
29 Margaret Silf, *Landmarks: An Ignatian Journey*, Darton, Longman and Todd 1998, p. 127.

Chapter 6

1 Thomas à Kempis, *On the Imitation of Christ*, Oxford University Press 1929, p. 68.
2 William A. Barry, *Finding God in All Things*, Ave Maria Press 1991, p. 124.
3 Charles Elliott, *Praying the Kingdom*, Darton, Longman and Todd 1985, p. 32.
4 Elliott, *Praying the Kingdom*, p. 32.
5 Elliott, *Praying the Kingdom*, p. 32.
6 J. Moltmann, *The Crucified God*, SCM Press 1974, p. 34.
7 Moltmann, *The Crucified God*, p. 40.
8 Alan Jones, *Soul Making*, SCM Press 1985, p. 203.
9 Jones, *Soul Making*, p. 203.
10 See for example, J. Krall and J. Kalberer, *Finding the Clown in Yourself*, Resource Publications Inc. 1987.

11 Ann and Barry Ulanov, *The Witch and the Clown*, Chiron Publications 1987, p. 211.
12 Patrick Forbes, *The Gospel of Folly*, Angel Press 1988, p. 17.
13 Harvey Cox, *The Feast of Fools*, Harper and Row 1969, p. 155.
14 Forbes, *The Gospel of Folly*, p. 49
15 A.V. Campbell, *Rediscovering Pastoral Care*, Darton, Longman and Todd 1981, p. 54.
16 Roly Bain, *Fools Rush In*, Marshall Pickering 1993, p. 79.
17 Henri J.M. Nouwen, *Clowning in Rome*, Image Books 1979, p.104.
18 M. Liebenow, *Is There Fun After Paul?*, Resource Publications Inc. 1987, p. 46.
19 Nouwen, *Clowning in Rome*, p. 2.
20 Forbes, *The Gospel of Folly*, p.19.
21 Forbes, *The Gospel of Folly*, p.107
22 Erasmus, *Praise of Folly*, Penguin Classics 1971, p. 152. A recent book which among other things gives an account of laughter in the Old Testament and the New Testament and discusses the Christian's ambiguity towards laughter in: M.A. Screech, *Laughter at the Foot of the Cross*, Penguin 1997.
23 Screech, *Laughter*, p. 185.
24 Screech, *Laughter*, p. 198.
25 Bain, *Fools Rush In*, p. 49
26 Liebenow, *Is There Fun After Paul?*, p. 35
27 Gerard W. Hughes, *O God, Why?*, The Bible Reading Fellowship 1993, p. 148.
28 Jones, *Soul Making*, p. 154.
29 Jones, *Soul Making*, p. 48.
30 Kahlil Gibran, *The Prophet*, Heinemann Ltd 1980, p. 16.
31 Gibran, *The Prophet*, p. 20.
32 Jones, *Soul Making*, p. 92.
33 Moltmann, *The Crucified God*, p. 62.
34 T. Jasper and M. Blyth, *In Unexpected Places*, Marshall Pickering 1988, p. 67.

Chapter 7

1 Antoine de Saint-Exupéry, *The Little Prince*, Mammoth Press 2001, p. 68.
2 Malcolm A. Rothwell, *The Selection of Candidates for the Church of Scotland Ministry*, unpublished PhD thesis, Edinburgh 1975, p. 146.
3 Rothwell, *The Selection of Candidates*, p. 146.
4 Petru Dumitriu, *To the Unknown God*, Collins 1982, p. 100.

5 Thomas Merton, *Contemplative Prayer*, Darton, Longman and Todd 1973, pp.83–4.
6 *The Cloud of Unknowing*, Penguin, 1961, p. 60.
7 Brenda Boyle, *Meditations with Julian of Norwich*, Bear and Company 1983, p.71.
8 H. Backhouse (ed.), *The Dark Night of the Soul*, Hodder and Stoughton 1988, p. 105.
9 Simone Weil, *Waiting on God*, Fontana Religious 1959, p. 44.
10 Hans Urs von Balthasar, *On Prayer*, SPCK 1973, p. 105.
11 Dumitriu, *To the Unknown God*, p. 104.
12 Quoted in John Drury, *The Pot and the Knife*, SCM Press 1979, p. 72.
13 Rubem A. Alves, *The Poet, the Warrior, the Prophet*, SCM Press 1990, p. 100.
14 Alves, *The Poet . . .* , p. 101.
15 Martin Buber, *I And Thou*, T and T Clark 1984.
16 Alves, *The Poet . . .* , p. 18.
17 *Hymns and Psalms* 710.
18 Quoted in David Hay, *Exploring Inner Space*, Penguin 1982, p. 118.
19 William James, *The Varieties of Religious Experience*, Longmans, Green and Co. 1925, p. 511.
20 James, *Varieties of Religious Experience*, p. 515.
21 Dumitriu, *To the Unknown God*, p. 98.
22 Quoted in Simon Bailey, *The Well Within*, Darton, Longman and Todd 1996, p. 14.
23 Quoted in Carlos Valles, *Mastering Sadhana*, Fount 1991, p. 121.
24 Alan Jones, *Soul Making*, SCM Press, 1985, p. 21.
25 Brenda Lealman and Edward Robinson, *Knowing and Unknowing*, Christian Education Movement 1981, p. 42.

Chapter 8

1 D. Lonsdale, *Eyes to See, Ears to Hear*, Darton, Longman and Todd 1990, p. 65.
2 Peter Morea, *In Search of Personality*, SCM Press 1997, p. 180.
3 Jules J. Toner, *Discerning God's Will*, Institute of Jesuit Sources 1991, p. 26.
4 Lonsdale, *Eyes to See*, p. 64.
5 Toner, *Discerning God's Will*, p. 28.
6 # indicates the appropriate paragraph in Louis J. Puhl, *The Spiritual Exercises of Ignatius Loyola*, Loyola University Press 1951; ## indicates the appropriate paragraph in George E. Ganss, *Ignatius of*

Loyola, Spiritual Exercises and Selected Works, The Classics of
Western Spirituality, Paulist Press 1991.

7   William A. Barry and William J. Connolly, *The Practice of Spiritual Direction*, Harper 1992 p. 102.

8   William A. Barry, *Spiritual Direction and the Encounter with God*, Paulist Press 1992, p. 75.

9   John J. English, *Spiritual Freedom*, Loyola University Press 1995, p. 18.

10 English, *Spiritual Freedom*, p. 18

11 The Methodist covenant service was instigated by John Wesley. He drew heavily on the puritan writings of Joseph and Richard Alleine but it is not easy to say whether he had any knowledge of Ignatius. In fact Sheldrake asserts, 'I have not found any evidence of the assertion' that 'Wesley knew of the Spiritual Exercises and was familiar with imaginative scripture prayer'. See, *The Way Supplement, Ignatian Spirituality in Ecumenical Context*, no. 68, Summer 1990.

12 See article on 'Indifference' in *Dictionary of Christian Spirituality*, Gordon S. Wakefield (ed.), SCM Press 1989, p. 213.

13 *Dictionary of Christian Spirituality*, p. 212.

14 Anthony de Mello, *Awareness*, Fount 1990, p. 134.

15 de Mello, *Awareness*, p. 118.

16 Carlos Valles, *Mastering Sadhana*, Fount 1991, p. 53.

17 David Hay, *Exploring Inner Space*, Penguin 1982, p. 118.

18 Lonsdale, *Eyes to See*, p. 71.

19 David Lonsdale, *The Serpent's Tail*, Supplement to the Way, no. 52 1985.

20 Lonsdale, *Eyes to See*, p. 71.

21 English, *Spiritual Freedom*, p. 181.

22 Carlo-Maria Martine, *Letting God Free Us*, St Pauls 1993, p. 119.

23 Martine, *Letting God Free Us*, p. 117.

24 Lonsdale, *Eyes to See*, pp. 80–1.

25 Gerard W. Hughes, *God, Where Are You?*, Darton, Longman and Todd 1997, p. 173.

26 Martine, *Letting God Free Us*, p. 117.

27 Hughes, *God, Where Are You?*, p. 214.

Chapter 9

1   Herbert Alphonso, *The Personal Vocation*, Centrum Ignatianum Spiritualitatis, 1990, p. 36.

2   William A. Barry and William J. Connolly, *The Practice of Spiritual Direction*, Harper Collins p. 48.

3 See for example, Norvene Vest, *Knowing by Heart*, Darton, Longman and Todd 1993.

4 Vest, *Knowing by Heart*, p. 3.

5 Carlos Valles, *Mastering Sadhana*, Fount 1991, p. 88, exercise 22.

6 Anthony de Mello, *Sadhana: A Way to God*, Gujarat Sahitya Prakash 1991, p. 91.

7 *To a Mouse, On Turning up her Nest with the Plough* in *Burns: Poems and Songs*, James Kinsley (ed.), Oxford University Press 1971.

8 Petru Dumitriu, *To the Unknown God*, Collins 1982, p. 48.

9 Maurice Nicoll, *The New Man*, Shambhala 1986, p. 20.

10 Scholars are divided as to the precise ending of Mark's Gospel. Ancient manuscripts differ.

11 T. Jasper, *Living Words for Now*, SPCK 1978, p. 187.

Chapter 10

1 Ann and Barry Ulanov, *The Witch and the Clown*, Chiron Publications 1987, p. 200.

2 P. Forbes, *The Gospel of Folly*, Angel Press 1988, p. 37.

3 M. Liebenow, *Is There Fun After Paul?*, Resource Publications Inc. 1987, p. 48. See also Colin Morris, *The Hammer of the Lord*, Epworth Press 1973 which has a chapter on 'A symbol of hope – the clown'.

4 Lewis Carroll, *The Complete Works of Lewis Carroll*, Penguin 1988, p. 148.

Select bibliography

Simon Bailey, *The Well Within*, Darton, Longman and Todd 1996.

Roly Bain, *Fools Rush In*, Marshall Pickering 1993.

Hans Urs von Balthasar, *On Prayer*, SPCK 1973.

William A. Barry, *Finding God in All Things*, Ave Maria Press 1991.

William A. Barry, *Spiritual Direction and the Encounter with God*, Paulist Press 1992.

William A. Barry and William J. Connolly, *The Practice of Spiritual Direction*, Harper Collins 1982.

Alastair V. Campbell, *Rediscovering Pastoral Care*, Darton, Longman and Todd 1981.

Alastair V. Campbell, *The Gospel of Anger*, SPCK 1986.

J.-P. de Caussade, *The Sacrament of the Present Moment*, Collins 1981.

Anthony de Mello, *Awareness*, Fount 1990.

Petru Dumitriu, *To the Unknown God*, Collins 1982.

Charles Elliott, *Praying the Kingdom*, Darton, Longman and Todd 1985.

John J. English. *Spiritual Freedom*, Loyola University Press 1995.

Patrick Forbes, *The Gospel of Folly*, Angel Press 1988.

George E. Ganss, *Ignatius of Loyola, Spiritual Exercises and Selected Works,* The Classics of Western Spirituality, Paulist Press 1991.

David Hay, *Exploring Inner Space*, Pelican 1982.

Gerard W. Hughes, *God of Surprises*, Darton, Longman and Todd 1985.

Gerard W. Hughes, *God, Where Are You?*, Darton, Longman and Todd 1997.

Gerard W. Hughes, *O God, Why?*, The Bible Reading Fellowship 1993.

Alan Jones, *Soul Making*, SCM Press 1985.

Julian of Norwich, *Revelations of Divine Love*, Penguin Classics 1966.

Paul Lakeland, *Postmodernity, Christian Identity in a Fragmented Age*, Fortress Press 1997.

M. Liebenow, *Is There Fun After Paul?*, Resource Publications Inc. 1987.

David Lonsdale, *Eyes to See, Ears to Hear*, Darton, Longman and Todd 1990.

David and Vera Mace, *Love and Anger in Marriage*, Pickering and Inglis 1983.

Carlo-Maria Martine, *Letting God Free Us*, St Pauls 1993.

Thomas Merton, *Contemplative Prayer*, Darton, Longman and Todd 1973.

Thomas Merton, *The Wisdom of the Desert*, Sheldon Press 1974.

J. Richard Middleton and Brian J. Walsh, *Truth is Stranger than it Used to Be: Biblical Faith in a Postmodern Age*, SPCK 1995.

J. Moltmann, *The Crucified God*, SCM Press 1974.

Peter Morea, *In Search of Personality*, SCM Press 1997.

Dorothy Rowe, *Depression: The Way Out of Your Prison*, Routledge and Kegan Paul 1983.

John A. Sanford, *Ministry Burnout*, Arthur James Ltd 1982.

P. Sheldrake (ed.), *The Way of Ignatius Loyola*, SPCK 1991.

Margaret Silf, *Landmarks: An Ignatian Journey*, Darton, Longman and Todd 1998.

John Shelby Spong, *Why Christianity Must Change or Die*, Harper and Row 1998.

Anthony Storr, *Human Aggression*, Penguin 1968.

Jules J. Toner, *Discerning God's Will*, Institute of Jesuit sources 1991.

Ann and Barry Ulanov, *The Witch and the Clown*, Chiron Publications 1987.

Carlos Valles, *Mastering Sadhana*, Fount 1991.